Harvard Business Review

ON

DEVELOPING LEADERS

THE HARVARD BUSINESS REVIEW PAPERBACK SERIES

The series is designed to bring today's managers and professionals the fundamental information they need to stay competitive in a fast-moving world. From the preeminent thinkers whose work has defined an entire field to the rising stars who will redefine the way we think about business, here are the leading minds and landmark ideas that have established the *Harvard Business Review* as required reading for ambitious businesspeople in organizations around the globe.

Other books in the series:

Harvard Business Review Interviews with CEOs

Harvard Business Review on Advances in Strategy

Harvard Business Review on Becoming a High Performance Manager

Harvard Business Review on Brand Management

Harvard Business Review on Breakthrough Leadership

Harvard Business Review on Breakthrough Thinking

Harvard Business Review on Building Personal and Organizational Resilience

Harvard Business Review on Business and the Environment

Harvard Business Review on the Business Value of IT

Harvard Business Review on Change

Harvard Business Review on Compensation

Harvard Business Review on Corporate Ethics

Harvard Business Review on Corporate Governance

Harvard Business Review on Corporate Responsibility

Harvard Business Review on Corporate Strategy

Harvard Business Review on Crisis Management

Harvard Business Review on Culture and Change

Harvard Business Review on Customer Relationship Management

Harvard Business Review on Decision Making

Other books in the series (continued):

Harvard Business Review

ON

DEVELOPING LEADERS

A HARVARD BUSINESS REVIEW PAPERBACK

The *Harvard Business Review* articles in this collection are available as individual reprints. Discounts apply to quantity purchases. For information and ordering, please contact Customer Service, Harvard Business School Publishing, Boston, MA 02163. Telephone: (617) 783-7500 or (800) 988-0886, 8 A.M. to 6 P.M. Eastern Time, Monday through Friday. Fax: (617) 783-7555, 24 hours a day. E-mail: custserv@hbsp.harvard.edu

Library of Congress Cataloging-in-Publication Data
Harvard business review on developing leaders.
      p. cm. — (The Harvard business review paperback series)
    Includes index.
    ISBN 1-59139-500-3
    1. Executive ability. 2. Executives—Selection and appointment. 3. Executives—Training of. 4. Leadership. I. Harvard business review. II. Series.
    HD38.2.H3744 2004
    658.4′07124—dc22
                                            2003023489
                                                  CIP

Contents

Harvard
Business
Review

ON

DEVELOPING LEADERS

Are You Picking the Right Leaders?

MELVIN SORCHER AND JAMES BRANT

Executive Summary

WHEN IT COMES TIME TO HIRE or promote, top executives routinely overvalue certain skills and traits while overlooking others. Intuitively, for example, they might seek out team players, people who shine operationally, dynamic public speakers, or those who are demonstrably hungry for greater responsibility.

But some attributes that seem like good indicators of leadership potential are, paradoxically, just the reverse. Team players and those who excel operationally often make better seconds in command. Many a great public speaker lacks the subtle one-on-one persuasive powers that a top leader needs. And shows of raw ambition may be more an indicator of ego than of leadership talent.

Unfortunately, few organizations have the right procedures in place to produce complete and accurate pictures of their top prospects. Assessments are often based

1

on hearsay, gossip, and casual observation. Many companies spend too much effort trying to develop leaders and not enough effort trying to identify them.

A new evaluation process will help you avoid that trap. Candidates are assessed by a group of people who have observed their behavior directly over time and in different circumstances. Using a carefully crafted series of questions, the group can probe a wide range of leadership criteria, including such "soft" attributes as personal integrity, that are difficult to assess. Without such information, senior management will remain vulnerable to misidentifying leadership talent, and the wrong people will continue to make their way up the corporate ladder.

CEOS AND OTHER TOP EXECUTIVES know that one of their most important jobs is management succession, and they are well aware that the process of identifying potential leaders is neither simple nor straightforward. They fully realize that leadership is a complex, multifaceted capability, with myriad nuances and subtleties and that the characteristics that can help a person succeed in one environment (turning around a losing division, for instance) may lead to failure in another situation (such as starting up a new business). Despite this awareness and the best of intentions, many senior executives make the costly and painful mistake of tapping the wrong person for a key position.

In our experience helping companies predict which people are most likely to succeed in roles of broader responsibility, we have found that CEOs, presidents, executive vice presidents, and other top-level people often fall into the trap of making decisions about candidates based on lopsided or distorted information. Frequently, they fall prey to the "halo effect": overvaluing certain attributes while undervaluing others. They might, for instance, be drawn to a candidate's operational proficiency and considerable experience in a broad range of assignments while overlooking his extreme aversion to risk. To make matters worse, many organizations do not have the right procedures in place to produce a complete and accurate picture of their top prospects. All too often, assessments are based on hearsay, gossip, casual observation, and insufficient information.

To help overcome these problems, we have developed an evaluation process in which a candidate is assessed by a group of people, including the individual's manager and other executives, who have observed his or her behavior directly over time and in different circumstances. The process enables the group to probe a wide range of leadership criteria and obtain balanced and complete information. Think of it as an annual physical, which relies not just on a blood test for cholesterol but also on an EKG, an eye exam, a hearing check, and various other indicators to assess a person's overall general health. Such thorough and systematic evaluations will help senior executives avoid the pitfall of promoting the wrong people.

The Leadership Trap

Since the 1980s, we have worked extensively with large corporations to improve their CEO succession, assessment of senior executives, and early identification of leadership talent. We have experience with a variety of businesses and corporate cultures, including manufacturing, consumer products, high technology, and financial services, and we have assessed thousands of senior executives, including many CEO candidates. (For confidentiality, we have altered some of the details of the executives described in the examples.) In some cases, companies have completely reversed their opinions of candidates based on the information that surfaced during our evaluations, and we believe that serious and very costly mistakes have been avoided. (See "The Hardwiring of Leadership" at the end of this article.)

To assess a candidate properly, senior executives must consider the full range of leadership criteria, including the various "soft" skills and characteristics, such as personal integrity, that are difficult to judge. Furthermore, decisions should be based on an integrated view of the candidate drawn from the various perspectives held by the people who have managed and worked with the individual throughout his or her career. The evaluation processes at many organizations, however, do not produce such complete and accurate information, leaving senior executives vulnerable to various pitfalls when assessing candidates. One of the most fundamental mistakes is that tendency to overvalue certain characteristics, attributes, and skills:

BEING A TEAM PLAYER

People who manage by consensus often climb the corporate ladder quickly. Their bosses usually view them favorably because they make life easier by helping their divisions, departments, or groups run smoothly. After all, few senior executives enjoy spending their time playing peacekeeper or referee.

But we have found that such individuals do not make exceptional leaders. In fact, the best leaders are usually not team players; they feel little need to work in a group.

They might prefer *others* to work as a team and will give lip service to teams, but when push comes to shove they do not have any compelling need to listen to people's ideas fully before moving on. They are independent thinkers, and they don't mind making decisions by themselves, decisions that set them apart from the pack.

By contrast, consensus managers have trouble making a decision unless everyone is in general agreement with it—and this trait can become their undoing. Consider the executive hired to head a publishing company because of his solid track record as CEO of a consumer services company. He was very collaborative and always solicited other people's opinions and ideas. After he was hired at the publishing company, though, people became impatient with him because the organization seemed to lack a clear direction. In short, his vision—a key criterion for leadership—wasn't really his. It was more a mushy amalgam of other people's ideas, and he was slow in making decisions. An underlying reason for this hesitancy might have been an aversion to risk: He may have been afraid of moving forward without first building the consensus he thought was necessary. Not surprisingly, he was seen as indecisive, he couldn't win people's respect, and he consequently failed.

What's more, consensus managers tend to assemble teams of people who are like themselves. Homogeneous groups often run more smoothly, but they usually lack the synergistic power of a diverse team of people with talents, skills, and characteristics that complement one another. Exceptional leaders are willing to take risks by picking people who are unlike them—and who may even have different leadership styles. They are also willing to take a chance on untested people if they size them up and conclude they have what it takes. Furthermore, such leaders do not feel threatened when they hire someone who is more skilled, better experienced, and smarter than they are.

HANDS-ON COACHING

Another common misconception is that leaders actively try to develop others through close mentoring relationships. Many excellent leaders instead prefer to select strong people and delegate fully to them, providing them with various opportunities to grow through their own experiences and make their own fair share of mistakes. Good leaders do have an interest in developing others but not always through hands-on relationships.

OPERATIONAL PROFICIENCY

CEOs and other senior executives often overvalue people who are good implementers and problem solvers. As we've said, people who make their bosses' lives easy often do very well in an organization. Although good foot soldiers are an asset to any company, they often don't make effective leaders.

Sometimes, proficient individuals rely too heavily on systems, policies, and procedures, rigidly expecting everyone to operate in that same style. Such people can succeed in an organization until they rise to very senior positions, where their need for regimentation tends to alienate others and stifle innovation.

Superior problem-solving capabilities can also mask a deficiency in long-range, conceptual, or strategic thinking. Consider the classic story of the lieutenant who, after his captain orders, "Take that hill," promptly does so. But when the captain asks instead, "Of those seven

hills out there, which one should we take?" the lieutenant has no idea. Being able to solve a problem is one
thing; knowing which problem to solve—and then taking
the initiative to solve it—is quite another.

Many operational experts are good at tackling well-
defined problems, say, how to increase a mature product's profitability by 4%. But leaders must also be adept
at handling problems that are nebulous or ambiguous,
such as how to reposition that same product line (or
even whether to kill it off) when a new competitor enters
the market. The higher people rise in an organization,
the fewer facts they typically have to inform their decisions. Thus, an ability to handle—and even thrive in—ill-
defined and complex situations is critical. Many good
operations managers become confused and hesitant in
ambiguous circumstances, delaying their decisions until
they have 99% of the available facts. Others are prema-
turely decisive when they ought to be more reflective.
Exceptional leaders do neither: They are comfortable
acting in gray areas and, in fact, are often able to exploit
ill-defined and complicated situations to their advantage, seeing opportunity where others see only confusion. All too often, though, companies undervalue this
crucial ability—if they consider it at all.

What's more, results-oriented individuals who have
superior operational skills can easily fail in top executive
positions if they have major character flaws. For
instance, one executive we evaluated was extremely
effective in generating new business. He was an impressive rainmaker, responsible for a significant fraction of
the total revenues for his organization, a large manufacturing company. But he didn't share information with
peers and was considered overly competitive and manip-
ulative. Senior management tolerated his shortcomings

because he ran a profitable operation. Eventually, though, his lack of integrity—and the fact that his peers didn't trust him—prevented him from being considered for a top position.

Of course strong operational skills are invaluable, but the truth is that a person who is not experienced in all aspects of operations yet who excels at envisioning the future, taking prudent risks, and exploiting ambiguity can be a strong leader, particularly with the right support. We might recommend that such a candidate, if promoted, be paired with a number two person who has strong operational skills.

DYNAMIC PUBLIC SPEAKING

We have found that senior executives tend to overvalue how people comport themselves in front of others. In particular, they tend to put great weight on stand-up presentation skills. While these skills are certainly important, they can be developed through extensive coaching, and we have found that a deficiency here is rarely the reason for an executive's failure. A more difficult shortcoming to correct—and one that people sometimes minimize—is a lack of one-on-one social skills. Without the ability to engage, convince, and inspire others—not only large groups in public but also individuals in private settings—leaders will find it difficult to enlist the people they need to support their cause.

RAW AMBITION

A perceived lack of ambition has scuttled many a promotion. "I'm not sure how hungry she is" or "He seems to lack that fire in the belly" are common criticisms. Unfortunately, executives sometimes forget that a person's ambition can be understated. Indeed, we have found that many exceptional leaders are modest and display little ambition, even though on the inside they are fiercely competitive. In fact, a high degree of personal humility is far more evident among exceptional leaders than is raw ambition.

SIMILARITY AND FAMILIARITY

Many top executives tend to favor those with backgrounds, experiences, and characteristics similar to their own. Sometimes promising candidates are overlooked because of differences in race, gender, or socioeconomic, cultural, academic, or geographic background or because they have never held a comparable position at a similar company. But remarks such as "He doesn't fit in," or "The chemistry isn't quite there," or "She's not really part of our culture" should not automatically disqualify a candidate. They should instead prompt a probe for further details.

Even the most trivial factors sometimes come into play. At a *Fortune* 100 corporation, we were helping the chairman and CEO, who would soon both be retiring, to evaluate potential replacement candidates. Each had his own candidate in mind, but we instead recommended that they consider someone else for a combined role, a vice president who hadn't been at the company that long but who we felt had great potential. Both the chairman and CEO commented on the vice president's height, but we insisted they look beyond appearances. They eventually promoted him, and his track record at the helm was excellent. In another instance, a brilliant candidate was almost passed over because he was overweight and considered "disheveled."

Peeling the Leadership Onion

Many companies fail to develop a rounded picture of their leadership candidates because the processes they employ are inherently flawed. Typically, management reviews tend to focus on the performance of certain tasks, relying on a checklist of competencies, and fail to investigate the behavioral characteristics of an individual. And even when such information is considered, the full range of leadership criteria—particularly soft skills such as the ability to inspire others—is often not probed adequately. Frequently, individuals with superior potential are impaled on a single mistake, while mediocre ones are sometimes raised to great heights because they once got lucky.

To avoid the trap of overvaluing certain attributes while undervaluing others, we have developed an evaluation process that calls for a small group of people to get together and discuss the individual's history. Including the candidate's boss and other executives who have dealt directly with him or her over the years, the group examines a wide range of leadership criteria—everything from an ability to assemble a top-notch staff to the capacity for strategic thinking. Characteristics that are often taken for granted (a person's integrity, for instance) are probed with specific questions ("Have you ever known him to shade, color, or distort information to his advantage?"). Directing this discussion is an internal executive or a consultant.

Through a set of such carefully crafted questions, patterns in observed behavior are uncovered. (See "Knowing What to Look for—and How to Find It" at the end of this article.) People often see a hint of something that doesn't unduly bother them so they let it pass, or they have certain feelings that they haven't quite been able to articulate or confirm with other people. But when they hear others talking about a similar experience with or feelings about the candidate, the issue crystallizes. For example, we were once discussing an individual's integrity, and the person's former manager said to his current boss, "I just came across some recent information that I'll pass along to you later." But we urged the manager to share that information with the group. Very reluctantly, he did. Soon, the other participants were telling a similar story, and what emerged from the discussion was a pattern showing that the candidate frequently manipulated people and situations for his own benefit.

Conversely, participants in the group can often have opinions—based, perhaps, on a hunch or gut feeling—that are unfounded. In such cases, the discussion leader must probe for specific examples as evidence. Only direct observations are considered; secondhand information, hearsay, and rumors are quickly discounted. The discussion leader encourages everyone to add information, question one another, agree when they've observed similar behavior, and disagree when they've observed something different. (Usually the disagreements arise because the candidate behaves differently in different situations.) In our experience, any distorted information contributed by people with axes to grind will usually be corrected by others—another important benefit of the group evaluation process. The result is a view of the candidate that is typically more accurate, balanced, and richer than could be gotten if the person had been evaluated by each participant individually.

The group evaluation also helps cut through unfounded assumptions that may be dogging someone's career. For example, someone might say of one candidate, "She's great at getting results, but I don't believe that she can think strategically." Then the discussion leader would ask whether the candidate has ever been in a situation that required her to exercise that skill. If the answer is no, participants might decide to test the person by including her in a task force that requires her to anticipate problems, trends, and opportunities. Similarly, if someone says, "I think she'll be pretty good at strategic thinking" but is unable to provide direct evidence, then again the participants might decide to test the candidate in this area.

When an answer is vague (for example, "He's pretty good at figuring out how to resolve problems"), the discussion leader probes for specificity ("What would he have to do for you to say that he is an exceptional problem solver?"). The process is like peeling away the layers of an onion, as each question delves deeper than the last. (See "Getting to the Core of Leadership" at the end of this article for a sample excerpt from a group evaluation.)

The discussion leader also asks the participants a series of questions intended to predict how the candidate will perform in a position of greater responsibility. Without this element of prediction, the assessment process would not be all that useful for leadership development, but unfortunately, the review process at many organizations stops short of this step. In a group evaluation, the leader asks questions such as, "Based on how you've described this person and everything you've observed about her, how would you predict she will perform in a position of increased responsibility?" and "Specifically, if she were to fail, what would you predict might be the most likely reason or reasons?"

From this information, the group can determine development priorities for the candidate. If there's no evidence that the individual can, say, manage a geographically dispersed organization, the group might develop a plan that expressly requires her to do so. Details of this plan should include a specific time frame for the test, the criteria that will be used to determine success, and a list of the early warning signs of potential failure. To encourage the participants to give their honest views of the candidate, the discussion leader should emphasize that the ultimate goal of the group evaluation is to develop the individual and that information will be kept confidential. Furthermore, the dynamics and structure of the group organization reinforce candor and confidentiality.

At many organizations, much leadership talent goes untapped. Top executives identify the wrong people as having high potential, often because they work with incomplete or inaccurate information that leads them to overvalue certain capabilities and qualities. Candidates are sometimes promoted to key positions just because they possess one remarkable characteristic, such as excellent communication skills that can persuade and inspire others. Superior individuals may be weeded out because they do not wear their ambition on their sleeves.

No wonder, then, that many companies are struggling with a leadership shortage. We believe that leadership talent is more available than people think. The trick is to identify it properly, and doing so requires sorting through the myriad nuances and subtleties of leadership. At a minimum, organizations need an evaluation process that yields a full, balanced, and accurate picture of candidates. Without such information, senior management will remain vulnerable to misidentifying its leadership talent, and the wrong people will continue to make their way up the corporate ladder.

The Hardwiring of Leadership

OUR EXPERIENCE HAS LED us to believe that much of leadership talent is hardwired in people before they reach their early or mid-twenties. That means, as far as leadership is concerned, people are reasonably complete packages by the time they arrive at the corporate doorstep. Their ability to lead has already been shaped by a multitude of factors and experiences that took root early in their lives. Some of these experiences were within their control; many others were happenstance.

We have followed individuals at many organizations as their careers progressed and have found a remarkable stability and consistency in virtually all aspects of their behavior over time. Simply put, people do not change very much once they enter the corporate world, and the changes that do occur are mainly a matter of a consolidation of strengths—or a downward drift in behavior that needs improvement. For some fortunate individuals, all the elements of exceptional leadership are in place. For many others, formal development programs will not automatically transform them into superior leaders, as if they were butterflies emerging from cocoons.

Unfortunately, though, many companies tend to focus their energies on developing leaders rather than on accurately identifying them in the first place. We believe that corporate leadership development programs can certainly produce an abundance of better managers: They do a fine job of communicating standards, establishing expectations, and setting direction. But they are not effective corporate assembly lines for manufacturing exemplary leadership skills.

Knowing What to Look for—and How to Find It

EVALUATING A CANDIDATE for a senior-level position is a daunting task. Indeed, judging different individuals on such a multifaceted and nuanced capability as leadership is, at best, an imperfect process. That said, we have found that the best way to assess a person's capacity to lead is through a group evaluation that includes the individual's manager, his manager's manager, and several people senior to him who have worked with him directly. The leader of the discussion probes the candidate's characteristics and behavior by asking the group a set of questions covering a wide range of criteria. The following represents just a small sampling of questions one might ask of a particular candidate.

Describe the candidate's integrity:

- Have you ever known him to shade, color, or withhold information? If so, what were the circumstances?

- Does he give credit to others when appropriate?
- Does he stand firm in his opinions, or does he move with the winds of politics? Can you give examples?

Describe how the candidate communicates information and expectations:

- How persuasive is he in getting his ideas accepted?
- Does he command the respect and attention of senior executives?
- Does he tailor his message to the needs of his audience? Examples?
- Is he intellectually aggressive without offending?

Describe how the candidate reasons and analyzes issues:

- How well and how quickly can he assemble and integrate a diversity of information?
- Is he logical, and how does he demonstrate sound judgment?
- When confronted with an ambiguous or complex situation, does he procrastinate? Or does he make decisions too quickly? Give an illustration.
- Is he more of a tactical or a strategic thinker?
- Does he have a vision for the company, and has he demonstrated that he can move a business into new areas?
- How well does he anticipate trends and translate them into the organization's long-term objectives? Examples?

Describe how the candidate runs his immediate work team:

- Has he demonstrated the ability to assemble a good team? Explain.

- Is he threatened by people who are more experienced, smarter, or better technically?

- How well does he work with people who have different styles and skills?

- Does he always surround himself with strong people who will be candid and tell him what he needs to know instead of what he wants to hear?

- How does he motivate others to accomplish things independently of him? Can you give examples?

- Does he delegate authority and responsibility or just tasks?

- Is he sometimes needlessly interested in certain activities? Or does he perhaps have a tendency to relinquish too much authority to others?

Getting to the Core of Leadership

THE FOLLOWING IS AN EXCERPT that captures a typical group evaluation session, this one of Jack Cotrell, a candidate for promotion to vice president of marketing. The participants include Herb Guzman, Jack's immediate manager; Eric Vieau and Christina Flood, Jack's two previous managers; and Roger Warniers, a vice president of sales who has worked with Jack as an internal customer. Leading the evaluation is Linda Chung, senior vice president of human resources. Although the dialogue is fictional, it is based on an actual case, and this brief excerpt demonstrates how the group evaluation process helps crystallize an issue drawn from multiple perspectives.

Linda: Let's talk about Jack's ability to reason things through and his quality of judgment. What are your observations?

Herb: My experience is that he's a pretty smart guy. He's solid and you can depend on him. He doesn't make many mistakes.

Linda: Herb, you said "pretty smart." What does an exceptional person do that Jack doesn't?

Herb: Actually, I'm not quite sure what I meant by "pretty smart" because Jack's got terrific analytical skills. He has a very logical mind and is able to reason through problems quickly.

Christina: I agree that Jack's a great problem solver.

Linda: Christina, any other observations?

Christina: Let me think. Well, I did get this feeling sometimes that he could be a little laid-back or hesitant, especially when the issues weren't totally familiar to him.

Linda: Any specific examples of this behavior?

Christina: It's just a sense I got. Sorry, I know this is not very helpful, but you asked me so I told you.

Linda: Eric or Roger?

Eric: I think Jack's especially good working across functional boundaries to get things done. But listening to Christina here, I guess I did notice that although he's great at getting results, he's not always the first to identify problems coming down the pike.

Roger: I'd like to add that Jack has always gotten along well with my people—he's very responsive to our needs—but I do agree with some of the prior comments that he can sometimes be reactive rather than proactive.

Linda: Are there any types of situations in which this is true? Any examples?

Roger: Well, I suppose he tends to be reactive when things are complicated and not well defined. I remember when we were trying to reposition one of our products; the requirements for that project kept on changing almost daily. Jack was great at fighting all those fires, but it would have been better if he could have helped us anticipate some of those problems.

Herb: I never thought of it that way: Some people are really good at knowing what to ask, getting that information, and then taking the right steps to avoid future problems. I never really get the sense that Jack can do that.

Through further discussion, the group concluded that Jack must demonstrate better long-term thinking and initiative before being promoted to vice president of marketing, a position that would require him to anticipate trends, opportunities, and problems. But after having probed other leadership criteria, the group agreed that Jack had numerous strengths, including his strong interpersonal and collaborative skills, his ability to motivate teams, and his solid record of selecting top talent. So, Jack's next assignment—to head a group responsible for developing a marketing campaign targeting a fickle but potentially lucrative category of new customers—was designed to provide him with ample opportunity to demonstrate more conceptual and strategic thinking.

Originally published in February 2002
Reprint R0202F

Managing Away Bad Habits

JAMES WALDROOP AND TIMOTHY BUTLER

Executive Summary

WE'VE ALL WORKED WITH highly competent people who are held back by a seemingly fatal personality flaw. One person takes on too much work; another sees the downside in every proposed change; a third pushes people out of the way. At best, people with these "bad habits" create their own glass ceilings, which limit their success and their contributions to the company. At worst, they destroy their own careers.

Although the psychological flaws of such individuals run deep, their managers are not helpless. In this article, James Waldroop and Timothy Butler—both psychologists—examine the root causes of these flaws and suggest concrete tactics they have used to help people recognize and correct the following six behavior patterns:

The *hero*, who always pushes himself—and subordinates—too hard to do too much for too long. The *meritocrat,* who believes that the best ideas can and will be determined objectively and ignores the politics inherent in most situations. The *bulldozer,* who runs roughshod over others in a quest for power. The *pessimist,* who always worries about what could go wrong. The *rebel,* who automatically fights against authority and convention. And the *home run hitter,* who tries to do too much too soon—he swings for the fences before he's learned to hit singles.

Helping people break through their self-created glass ceilings is the ultimate win-win scenario: both the individual and the organization are rewarded. Using the tactics introduced in this article, managers can help their brilliantly flawed performers become spectacular achievers.

We've all worked with people who are star performers but have one serious personality shortcoming that makes life difficult for everyone, limits their effectiveness, and often proves to be their professional undoing. One person, for instance, constantly takes on too much work. Another scorns the behind-the-scenes politicking needed to win support for most projects. A third sees the downside in every proposed change. In the words of one executive we worked with, such people are "95% brilliant, 5% disaster."

We call these destructive behavior patterns "bad habits" as a shorthand way of referring to deep-rooted psychological flaws. In other words, we're not using the term to describe compulsions like smoking or nail biting. Nor are we applying it to people who—at one time or another—bully coworkers, struggle with self-doubt, or drive themselves too hard. No one is perfect; we all wrestle with demons and make mistakes. Instead, we're using the term to talk about employees whose psychological makeup translates into consistently problematic behavior. Their "bad habits" are a central part of their personalities and inform the way they behave from day to day. At best, such people create their own glass ceilings, limiting their success and their contributions to the company. At worst, these otherwise highly competent and valuable people destroy their own careers.

Although the psychological flaws of such individuals run deep, their managers are not helpless. There are tested, effective ways to help people recognize and correct their bad habits. Over the course of almost 20 years of research and practice as business psychologists and executive coaches, we have identified 12 discrete patterns of behavior, or habits, that lead to these career troubles. Managers have a greater degree of leverage helping people whose behavior fits the following six patterns:

The Hero always pushes himself—and, by extension, subordinates—too hard to do too much for too long.

The Meritocrat believes that the best ideas can and will be determined objectively and thus will always prevail because of their clear merit; ignores the politics inherent in most situations.

The Bulldozer runs roughshod over others in a quest for power.

The Pessimist focuses on the downside of every change; always worries about what could go wrong rather than considering how things could improve.

The Rebel automatically fights against authority and convention.

The Home Run Hitter tries to do too much too soon —in other words, swings for the fences before he's learned to hit singles.

Let's be clear: we're not urging managers to get advanced degrees in psychology or to put their employees on the couch. But like it or not, managing today involves more than shuffling the right bodies on the assembly line; it requires knowledge of minds and hearts. Your only choice is between being a good "psychologist" or a bad one.

Being a good psychologist doesn't mean you have to explore your employees' complicated past to figure out exactly why they act the way they do. In fact, if an employee tells you "it all began when I was abused as a child," it's time to call in a professional. But you can use proven tactics to help the hero, the bulldozer, the pessimist, and the others become much more effective employees.

Our emphasis is on the practical. We have written in the past about retaining top talent. This article focuses on helping your star performers be most effective.

Helping people break through their self-created glass ceilings is one of the ultimate win-win scenarios you will encounter as a manager. When a member of your team reaches his or her potential, both the person and the organization are rewarded. We understand that this work requires precious time and energy on your part, but we're confident that the benefit to your organization will provide a better return than many other investments you could have made with your time. (Sometimes, however, it's better not to make the investment. Not everyone will respond, and it takes an ongoing effort. To perform a preliminary ROI analysis, see "Is It Worth the Effort?" at the end of this article.)

Root Causes

We have deliberately described the bad habits in our typology in simple, concrete terms. But it's useful to know a bit about the fundamental psychological processes underlying these behaviors. They grow out of a mix of an individual's genes and environmental influences, such as family and peer relationships. In one combination or another, these processes come together and lead some people into destructive behavior patterns. As a manager, you need only keep the processes in the back of your mind. Your goal isn't to offer counseling but to help your employees control the specific behaviors threatening to destroy their careers. You'll find that this objective is quite ambitious enough.

The four psychological processes underlying the bad habits are:

An inability to understand the world from the perspective of other people. An astonishing number of people have difficulty getting outside their own frame of reference and seeing through another person's. In other words, they lack empathy. In a sense, they never moved beyond the narcissism that is normal in childhood; they never got the instruction from parents or others that helps most people learn to understand the world from other people's perspectives. Having a well-developed sense of empathy is essential if one is to deal successfully with one's peers, subordinates, managers, customers, and competitors.

A failure to recognize when and how to use power. Many people feel a deep ambivalence about the utility and value of power. These feelings often stem from unconscious fears of our capacity for destructiveness. The fact is, many people confuse using power with abusing it. As a result, they either avoid gaining power altogether or they acquire it but then fail to use it—and power is a "use it or lose it" phenomenon. Of course, there are some people who are all too happy to obtain power, which they then wield like a cudgel instead of a surgeon's knife. In short, a great many businesspeople haven't done the hard work of figuring out how to use power effectively.

A failure to come to terms with authority. Most of us are ambivalent about authority. As children, for example, we often rebel against our parents even as we want to remain under their protection. Some people get stuck at one of the extremes. At one end are those who defy authority in every possible instance and in every possible way. At the other end are those who are overly deferential: "If top management says it's true, it must be." Most people fall somewhere in between. For example, in our experience, people like the idea of having a mentor but rebel when they actually have one.

A negative self-image. Poor self-esteem can come from various factors. Some people feel pressure from our achievement-driven culture to accomplish more—and to do it faster—than their peers. The possibility of failure is always looming. Other people's self-esteem deficiencies stem from mild to moderate levels of depression. Whatever the deep-seated reasons, building a career on a foundation of poor self-esteem is equivalent to erecting a skyscraper on sandy soil.

And yet, this psychological flaw undermines the confidence of a surprising number of businesspeople, from first-time managers to CEOs. One CEO of a successful high-tech firm who had unconsciously set himself up to be fired later admitted that he just never felt like he belonged "with the real grown-ups." It's not that he—or anyone—should always feel invincible. The goal is to be able to act effectively while accepting your inevitable shortcomings and life's disappointments.

That goal, in fact, is what drives our advice on how to help flawed performers overcome their bad habits. We'll look closely at each behavior pattern in turn.

The Hero

The hero is often the last person a manager wants to change. After all, why would you want to tamper with the behavior of someone who gets more done in a day than anyone else does in a week? The answer is that over the long term, the hero's constant pushing adds real costs to the bottom line—even if those costs are obscured by short-term results. If you look carefully at the hero's trail, you'll probably find the footprints of valuable people who left the company after trying to keep up with the hero's superhuman exertions. Within the company, you'll find burned-out coworkers. And the hero himself may be thoroughly spent, too.

People who habitually push themselves and others to the breaking point do so for various reasons. Some heroes become addicted to success at a very early age; others push and push as a way of dealing with their own shaky self-esteem. An "I'm gonna show them" mentality vis-à-vis authority is common. Clearly, heroes lack the empathy needed to understand what others are going through to keep up the pace.

To change a hero's behavior, start by expressing your appreciation for his accomplishments. But don't linger on that point—quickly segue into a discussion about the costs of burnout. Talk with the hero about recognizing the signs of overload in himself and in his team members. Make it clear that this is a very serious problem—that the hero has consistently taken things to a point at which more is not better. He needs to put on the brakes.

The hero must learn how important it is to take regular readings of his team's temperature. There are obvious physical cues: bags under the eyes, stifled yawns. In meetings, heroes need to learn to pay attention to body language, facial expressions, and energy levels that subtly indicate resistance or dismay.

As the hero's manager, you may want to help him make a checklist of warning signs that the temperature is getting too hot. The list might include the times that he and others are leaving voice messages and e-mails, the number of cars in the parking lot after 9 PM, rising levels of illness among employees (especially the number of people who come in even when they're sick), and reports of marital troubles. The hero should fill out the list weekly and discuss it with you.

Heroes have to think more about winning the war and less about the individual battles. A good general knows when to pull back to fight another day. Accordingly, you should reward the hero for actions that demonstrate a long-term focus and reprimand him for going to short-term extremes. We know of one case, for example, in which a hero was taken to task for making his team come in over the Fourth of July weekend. Emphasize that you need your hero to make strategic decisions; he should delegate the implementation whenever possible. You might encourage him to hire an assistant with both the confidence and the mandate to rein him in when he is driving too hard.

If your hero regularly intrudes on subordinates' time at home, you may need to ban him from contacting them at night or on weekends. If that seems unduly strict, you could require him to make explicit that he doesn't expect a response until the next day or after the weekend.

Finally, it is essential that someone take on the official role of observing the hero. The goal in dealing with this bad habit is to turn down the volume without switching it off. That's why you need someone with normal hearing to help the hero adjust the level. You could decide to do this yourself at least part of the time. Even so, it's a good idea to solicit another view. You can help your hero choose a trusted coworker to carry out this task. At least initially, that person should help the hero take his team's temperature. Most people are reluctant to tell the hero directly that they're tired and need a break.

Changing heroes' behavior is a delicate proposition. After all, you want heroes to continue to do all the good things they've been doing. At the same time, you have to let them know that there's nothing heroic about driving themselves and others into the ground. Careful "fine tuning" of these important contributors is essential.

The Meritocrat

Meritocrats earnestly believe that the world is a fair market in which the best ideas will always win on their own merit. Such people typically excelled at school. They were the outstanding test takers who were consistently rewarded for getting the highest score; thus they have a naïve reliance on the authority of objective, measurable facts. They never accepted that in the real world, ideas have to be sold, negotiated, and shaped to meet political and organizational realities. You have to be willing to horse-trade and to accept solutions that don't give you everything you want. People who don't accept these basic facts won't be as effective as they could be—in any situation.

Hal, for example, was an equities analyst at a New York investment bank. He was a quantitative whiz—he could tear apart a balance sheet faster and better than anyone else on the floor. But he would seethe when people challenged his analysis of a company or ignored his recommendations, especially when they acted only on their gut feel for the market. Likewise, when less bright but more politically savvy peers were promoted ahead of him, Hal was infuriated. These reactions, of course, were part of the reason he wasn't promoted. Hal's meritocratic behavior sabotaged his career.

To help a meritocrat, you should first offer sympathy. Go ahead and agree that it's really an awful waste of time to have to persuade people to support ideas of clear merit, to have to trade your quid for their quo, to tiptoe around certain sleeping dogs while throwing meat to others—and most of all, that it's too bad that we even have to spend our time having this discussion. In an ideal world, personal feelings and loyalties would have no place in decision making.

The next step is to raise a very difficult, but very important, question: how effective do you want to be? We've done this ourselves by using Jimmy Carter as an example. Carter, we say, was a highly principled and intelligent president who stayed unswervingly true to his ideals. And yet even the most die-hard Democrat would agree that Ronald Reagan was more effective than Carter at winning congressional and public support for his agenda. We ask, "Do you want to be 100% pure, like Carter, or do you want to be effective, like Reagan? You must choose one or the other."

Why even bother having this conversation? Because meritocrats are typically among your hardest-working, brightest, and most well-educated people. A manager needs to help them see that it is possible to operate in gray areas, accomplish a great deal, and still emerge relatively unsullied—say, 90% pure.

Give the meritocrat a little time to absorb this message, but don't let him drown in self-pity. Instead, jump to something concrete: "So, let's turn to that great initiative you mentioned to me last week. Let's do it. Who do we need to get on board to accomplish your goal? Whose opposition do we need to neutralize? What trade-offs do we have to make? How can we sell the idea to the final decision maker? Is there anything we should ask for now with the intention of giving up later?" And so on.

The point is to communicate that the business of actually getting things done is exciting and challenging—it's playing a game where the results really matter. Nothing is quite as satisfying as feeling personally effective, and that is what the meritocrat—with all his line-in-the-sand bravado—is likely to have missed out on. Once he has a taste of success, he'll usually want another—and the second time around it will all come more naturally to him.

Like the hero, the meritocrat has to learn much more about his team. For each member, he needs to ask himself, What does this person work for—big money, prestige, intellectual challenge, acquisition of power? What does this person most like to do—solve problems, think about the big picture, call the shots? And how does this person work—with attention to detail, by intuition, by networking, or alone in a quiet space? Only when the meritocrat understands and takes into account individual differences can he figure out how to get people to support his goals and make their strongest contribution to a project.

Understanding and accepting the personal factors that influence decision making is difficult at first. As the meritocrat's manager, you need to help him begin to see them objectively, as no different from any other factors being considered. Not everyone will come around to that view, of course. Some will prefer to move on to other places in search of a true meritocracy. Ultimately, however, the thrill of victory will be enough to persuade all but the most intractable meritocrats to change their behavior.

The Bulldozer

Bulldozers are people who decided early on that the world is a hostile place where you should do unto others before they do unto you—plus 10%. They intimidate and alienate everyone in their path. They don't trust others, and others don't trust them. At the same time, they're extremely loyal to their bosses, and they get things done—which is why they're worth trying to help.

Bulldozers are often reluctant to change a style that, by their lights, is highly effective. So to change a bulldozer, you have to become one yourself. Start by asking him if he has any idea how many enemies he has created within the company. Follow this with a powerful line we've used in our consulting: "If I put it to a vote, there's no question—you'd be fired."

A bulldozer will protest that you're being unfair. The right response is: "Look, I don't care if you think you're the gentlest person on earth. It doesn't even matter if I agree, because other people don't. And it's like being a stand-up comedian—if you think you're funny but the audience doesn't, you're not."

It helps to have some concrete evidence: "Did you notice in the meeting yesterday that after you finished questioning Joanne, no one said a word?" or "Here are some ways people describe you: cruel, mean-spirited, somebody I would never turn my back on." (We've heard all these comments made about bulldozers.) To get past a bulldozer's denial, it's often necessary to deliver the ultimate message: "I'm not going to baby you. You're costing me too much. Change or find another job."

The threat of being fired is usually quite motivating. If the bulldozer now indicates that he's willing to listen, the next step is to begin a campaign of rapprochement. Tell the bulldozer to make a list of his victims—people he has angered in the company. If he stumbles—if the list is too short—help him complete it. The bulldozer should then rank them from most damaged to least. Choosing the least-offended person first—in other words, the easiest to confront—the two of you should then script out (literally, on paper) an apology that *must* contain the words "I'm sorry."

Trivial as this may sound, it is essential that apologies be made for past misdeeds; and it will not be easy. To get your bulldozer used to saying the magic words, offer to role-play the part of the person he is going to try to make peace with. The odds are that the list of people deserving apologies is a long one, so he will get plenty of practice, but the first step is always the hardest. Offering apologies en masse won't smooth over all the damage, but it's a necessary first step.

The ultimate goal, of course, is to get the bulldozer to avoid causing damage in the first place. To do that, he has to become more aware of when he is about to roll over someone—what muscles tense up, what thoughts start to run through his head—so he can stop himself. He may have to take a break during a meeting or, in a conversation with an individual, pretend to have just remembered a call he has to make. These simple tactics actually work.

Your initial confrontation of a bulldozer needs to be strong and direct. It's also important to confront a bulldozer as soon as possible after seeing him in action; he'll start to recognize internal cues if you can point out external actions when they are still fresh in his mind. (This goes for all the bad habits. Like the clues in a crime scene, people's memories fade quickly. Time is your enemy when you're trying to help someone reconstruct what happened.) As with a hero, it's a good idea at the beginning to agree on someone the bulldozer trusts to monitor his behavior. If the bulldozer shows a willingness to change, he'll be able to build roads for you without flattening people in his way.

The Pessimist

Pessimists have nothing but the best intentions. Their goal is to preserve the organization from the harm that could come to it because of ill-advised change. The problem is, pessimists think *every* change is ill advised.

Pessimists' worries are sometimes justified—they're based on a knowledge of mistakes that others have made in the past. More frequently, though, pessimists simply stifle creativity and block fruitful opportunities. They also tend to micromanage, looking over everyone's shoulders lest a mistake be made.

Pessimists are motivated primarily by a fear of shame—of being wrong or inadequate. And avoidance of shame can spread insidiously throughout an organization's culture, becoming an unconscious modus operandi that has disastrous results for the company's capacity to innovate and take risks.

Fortunately, there are tactics that managers can use to change the pessimist's nay-saying. Begin by telling the pessimist that you're on his side in looking at proposals for change with appropriate caution. That positioning lets you avoid a pointless wrangle over the pros and cons of any particular initiative. Then point out that, as in the children's story of the boy who cried wolf, you're afraid that the impact of his alarms is diminishing. Moreover, he's giving the other members of his group a free ride: "They don't have to worry, and they certainly don't have to express their reservations. They've delegated that to you." The message is, it's okay to worry, but it's important that your fears do more than guard the status quo; they should have a constructive edge.

One way to make the pessimist's worry into a more effective tool is to teach him how to evaluate risk better. Pessimists not only ignore the potential upside of change, they also usually fail to consider the downside of doing nothing. Tell your pessimist that in the future, when a change initiative is proposed, he should draw a two-by-two matrix that looks at the pros and cons of making the change as well as the pros and cons of doing nothing. By making this systematic consideration of initiatives into a routine, the pessimist will be forced into a more objective risk analysis.

As a final step, you could offer to protect the pessimist from every kind of risk except one. Consider this example. One of our clients, an executive at a commercial bank, used almost those exact words to help a subordinate who said no at every opportunity. Our client finally said to him, "Look, we've got to take some risk when we lend money—that's why we get interest!" He helped the subordinate think about risk in a new way by telling him this: "If you try something new and fail, I'll take the blame. If you try something new and succeed, you'll get the credit. But if I find that you're refusing to take risks or getting in the way of others who have good ideas, you'll be held accountable." The pessimist got the message and learned to look at risk with more clarity.

In chess, fighting every game to a draw is not the objective; the goal is to checkmate your opponent. The pessimist must understand that you are playing to win, not to stay even. There are no draws in today's economy.

The Rebel

Teenagers imagine that they are rebelling by wearing funky clothes and getting outrageous haircuts. In reality, most are simply conforming to the look of their peers. Workplace rebels can also be quite conventional in their knee-jerk reactions against the status quo. Although they fancy themselves as revolutionaries, most of their protests against "the system" don't go beyond simple grousing—they rarely take action to change the things that bother them.

Rebels are easy to recognize. They're the ones who always ask the inappropriate questions in meetings, constantly make jokes about the company's management, and publicly question the motives behind any major change. Their cubes are papered with Dilbert cartoons, and their adherence to company rules is always just to the letter, never to the spirit. In short, rebels do enough to threaten morale that an effort to correct their behavior, assuming that they are otherwise valuable to the company, is a necessity.

What rebels enjoy most is a game of tug of war. So your first tactic is to refuse to play. Don't lose your temper; don't respond to provocation. You can then use two approaches to help the rebel break out of his negative behavior pattern.

The first is to co-opt the rebel by making him responsible for a relatively high-profile task that requires him to win the cooperation of others. In essence, you pull him out of the heckling audience and push him on stage, into the spotlight. The chance to take on an interesting and important project is, essentially, a bribe. Some rebels will see it as such but will take it anyway. Others will stubbornly refuse—in which case, on to the second approach.

Begin by asking the rebel, in a neutral tone and without warning, if he's thinking about quitting. When he— in a state of shock now—says no, tell him that you were wondering because he always seems to be butting up against the limits, venting his frustration, and putting the organization down. If he responds with "No, that's just my way of talking; I'm only kidding around," come back forcefully: "I don't buy that. And in any event, the things you say hurt people and the morale of the group. That needs to stop."

Then shift to a different gear: "But more to the point, you seem to think that a lot of things around here should be changed. True?" The rebel is likely to give some kind of affirmative response. At that point, throw down a challenge: "Well, right now you're about as effective a revolutionary as my three-year-old. All I have to do is tell him *not* to do what I actually want him to do, and he does it. And vice versa. Now, if you're going to battle the counterproductive aspects of the 'regime,' do you want to do it effectively, like a real guerrilla? Or do you just want to be the one who makes an impassioned speech before he gets dragged off to the firing squad?"

The latter is an unappealing option, so now you have the chance to help your rebel become a real leader of change. His first assignment should be to spend a week or two as a cultural anthropologist, noting all the subtle elements of your organization's culture: the way people dress and speak to one another; how much they reveal about their personal lives; how they align in groups; how decisions are made officially and how they are really made; who has informal power and influence, and so on. You should require him to hand you a written report at the end of this period.

Once the rebel has gathered that information, ask him this: "If you were a real revolutionary fighting somewhere against a dictatorship, would it be better to stand out or to blend in?" The answer is clear, so push the rebel to the logical conclusion. "You have a choice. You can work to change things here or you can follow your old pattern and just be an irritant. If you choose the latter, your career will stall and your influence on the organization will never amount to much. I hope you make the other choice, because you're right—this place isn't perfect, and we need people like you to help improve it."

The story of Charlotte, a young manager who was hired at a large insurance company, illustrates our point. She was appalled by the condescending attitude that senior management displayed toward the rank and file. Her response was to tweak the nose of the institution by dressing much more casually than other managers and taking her lunches with the frontline workers. When her manager discussed her behavior with her, Charlotte determined that she wanted to work to change the company's culture. And she did. Instead of "acting out" by dressing down, she directly confronted peers about their superior attitudes. (Ultimately, however, she found the pace of change too slow and moved on to work in another industry.)

A rebel who genuinely cares about the company (and his career) will see the light. Instead of being negative just for its own sake, he'll turn his energies toward constructive criticism and the building of a better company. He won't change overnight, and for some time you'll have to keep a close eye on the situation through frequent meetings. The payoff will make it worthwhile, however.

The Home Run Hitter

The home run hitter is the person who is always imagining the roar of the crowd when the ball clears the outfield fence. In business terms, he imagines his picture on the cover of *Fortune* as the founder of the hottest dot-com, or he sees himself making partner in record time by landing the biggest client. The problem is—going back to baseball—the home run hitter tends to strike out a lot, swinging for the fence when a simple base hit (or even a walk) would have helped the team just as much. Put simply, home run hitters focus on things that are too big too soon.

As a home run hitter's manager, you need to deliver two messages. Number one, you appreciate his drive, ambition, and self-confidence. Number two, you want to move him up the curve as quickly as possible but at a pace that ensures his steady progress.

Your home run hitter should understand that you're not holding him back because his abilities are suspect. In fact, you already see him as very successful—and right on track. Of course he wants to be at the top now; that's only natural for a high achiever. But you have confidence that he will get there if he stays with the program.

The next step is to explain just what the program is. It might include spending time overseas, working more with particular clients, and getting involved with the company's Web initiatives. It's useful to look at people in positions that he aspires to and explain their career trajectories; that way, he'll understand that they didn't just walk in off the street and take over.

Home run hitters worry that they'll never get ahead, and they feel that their strenuous efforts to reach the top go unappreciated. Therefore, it's important to talk with them often about their career progression and to praise them frequently—for small accomplishments as well as for large ones. Those actions on your part will help reassure your home run hitter that, given a little time, he'll have his shot at the big leagues.

John, for example, is a software engineer whose ambition and impatience were leading to bad choices. He was preparing to leave his current company—unwisely, we thought. We encouraged him to voice his concerns to his manager and to initiate more frequent "How am I doing?" meetings. Through those meetings, John gained a broader perspective, letting him see his manager's investment in his success. John just hadn't been able to visualize his career track. Armed with a new appreciation for the value of his work, he decided to stay with the company.

In an economy driven by the knowledge in people's heads, all good managers have to think like psychologists in order to maximize the potential of their people. You don't have to fix people's deep psychological problems, nor should you be trying. As a manager, your ultimate concern is with their actions and results. Although the tactics we recommend here won't work in every case (some people don't really want to change; others have damaged themselves too much within your organization to be salvageable), the approaches we describe are effective with many people. They can help turn your brilliantly flawed performers into spectacular achievers—to the benefit of themselves and your company.

Is It Worth the Effort?

BEFORE TRYING TO HELP ONE OF your flawed stars correct his bad habits, you need to make a crucial decision: is the person valuable enough to warrant the investment? In other words, Should you try to help him or should you "manage him out"?

To answer that question, consider the possible outcomes. The best-case and worst-case scenarios are fairly obvious. The most likely result, however, is that the person will take your cue and make an effort to change but will never altogether eradicate the problematic behavior. What is your threshold for a "good enough" recovery? At what point does the cost-benefit ratio move in your favor? Bear in mind that if you expect perfection, you are setting everyone up for failure.

You also need to ask yourself if you are the right person to try to help the employee change. Even if you recognize one of the behavior patterns in someone who reports to you, you may not feel comfortable dealing with it. Maybe you don't have the time or the energy; perhaps the person works off-site. In either case, you can get help from your HR department or from a highly experienced business psychologist or executive coach, both entirely acceptable responses.

If you want to go ahead on your own, plan the initial meeting carefully. Make sure you schedule enough time to discuss the situation thoroughly. You don't want to open up this topic unless you have the time to explore it fully.

It's important that you express clearly the reasons you believe your star performer falls into a particular behavior pattern. Make some notes beforehand so you can be specific and direct. Fresh, concrete evidence is best. For example, "In our meeting with Don, you interrupted him several times when he was explaining his concerns about your plan" or "I've asked you on three occasions now to sit down with Theresa and discuss her workload, but you haven't; you just keep piling it on her." You should also suggest some specific ideas to help the person change the behavior; these ideas will be fleshed out and modified during the conversation, but it's important to have a starting point. Finally, make time for a follow-up meeting soon after the initial discussion, preferably about a week later. Your work to help someone change a behavior pattern isn't a onetime operation. Bad habits take years to develop, and they won't change overnight.

Originally published in September 2000
Reprint R00512

Personalize Your Management Development

NATALIE SHOPE GRIFFIN

Executive Summary

MOST ORGANIZATIONS STRUGGLE with leadership development. They promote top performers into management roles, put them through a few workshops and seminars, then throw them to the wolves. Managers with the ability to survive and thrive are rewarded; those without it are disciplined or reassigned. The problem is, an alarming number of people fall into the second category. This happens not because managers lack skills but because companies fail to realize that there is no single kind of leader-in-training.

In this article, Natalie Shope Griffin, a consultant in executive and organizational development at Nationwide Financial, describes four kinds of managers-in-training, each embodying unique challenges and opportunities.

Reluctant leaders appear to have all the necessary skills to be excellent managers but can't imagine themselves succeeding in a leadership role.

Arrogant leaders have the opposite problem; they believe they already possess all the management skills they'll ever need.

Unknown leaders are overlooked because they don't develop relationships outside of a small circle of close colleagues.

Finally, there are the *workaholics* who put work above all else and spend 100 hours a week in the office.

The author outlines specific training approaches tailored to each type of prospective leader. By focusing on the unique circumstances of individual managers, investing in them early in their careers, offering effective coaching, and providing real-life management experiences, Nationwide's leadership-development program has produced hundreds of successful leaders.

$\mathbf{M}$OST ORGANIZATIONS STRUGGLE with leadership development. They promote their top performers into management roles, put them through a few workshops and seminars, and then throw them to the wolves. In the Darwinian process that follows, those with the ability to survive and thrive are rewarded; those without it are disciplined or reassigned. An alarming number of people fall into the second category.

Why do so many people botch their chances at success? It's not simply that new managers lack the talent or skills for the job. They fail, I've come to believe, because their companies' development approaches fail *them*. I've seen hundreds of leaders-in-training stumble as they attempt to master the difficult and subtle task of management. These prospective managers fall short because companies don't recognize the degree to which personal characteristics, ideologies, or behaviors affect an individual's ability to lead. The truth is, people don't check their individuality at the door before leaping into the great corporate melting pot, nor do they all fit a single leader-in-training profile.

At Nationwide Financial, a 5,000-employee financial services company based in Columbus, Ohio, we've found there are four kinds of people that land in management development programs, each embodying unique challenges and opportunities. First, there are the *reluctant leaders,* who appear to have all the necessary skills to be excellent managers but can't imagine themselves succeeding in a leadership role. *Arrogant leaders* have the opposite problem; they believe they already possess all the leadership skills they'll ever need. They typically lack the empathy and humility characteristic of an effective leader. The third group of people, *unknown leaders,* have the right blend of humility, confidence, and leadership skills, but their talents are overlooked because they fail to develop relationships outside of a small circle of close colleagues. Finally, there are the *workaholics,* the most common profile among our prospective managers. These individuals have been rewarded for putting work above all else and spending excessive hours at the office. Unfortunately, workaholics often lack both the perspective and personality to inspire others.

Identifying these four types of prospective managers and tailoring a specific development path for each has been a boon to Nationwide Financial. By treating potential leaders as individuals—focusing on their unique

personalities and circumstances, offering effective
coaching, and providing real-life management experiences—Nationwide's leadership development program
produced scores of effective managers during a time of
rapid growth and expansion when the company needed
leadership most.

Responding to the Pipeline Problem

In 1996, the leaders of Nationwide Financial's life insurance operations declared a state of management emer-
gency. Organizational structures had flattened during
the economic boom. As the remaining mid- and senior-
level managers were promoted or retired, those who
should have replaced them were increasingly unable to
lead. Employee satisfaction fell to low levels owing to
mediocre frontline management, which suffered from
discontent and turnover of its own. The morale problem
was exacerbated by the fact that Nationwide had been
forced into the expensive practice of hiring talented
managers from outside the company; employees hoping
for promotion felt passed over. It was clear the company
needed to develop a new generation of competent managers from within its own ranks.

To address this worrisome situation, a cross-
functional team (of which I later became a member) con-
ducted best-practice research into talent management
and leadership development and set about creating a
management development process. We agreed that only
a rigorously managed program committed to continuous
improvement would deliver the kinds of results the company hoped to see. The team opted to make application
to the program a matter of choice, rather than a prereq-
uisite for management positions; admission should be a

coveted prize so that participants would work hard during the development process. To that end, the admission process mimicked that of a top business school. In addition to submitting a portfolio of documents—performance evaluations, an essay, responses to a questionnaire, a recommendation from a manager—applicants would be screened and interviewed by a team of more senior managers and HR professionals.

The yearlong development program included coaching, mentoring, observing others, hands-on management experience, and training classes backed up by regular feedback sessions. The development focused on the whole person, not just on individual competencies. As the first rounds of participants moved through the program, we noticed that nearly all of them fell into one of four categories. Over the past five years, we've developed specific approaches tailored to each type of prospective leader.

The Reluctant Leader

About 20% of the participants in our program are "reluctant leaders." These employees often have the raw material to make outstanding managers, but they're sabotaged by their own lack of confidence. Their deeply ingrained insecurities manifest themselves in a variety of ways—indecisiveness, risk aversion, and the tendency to avoid conflict. To transform reluctant leaders into strong ones requires helping them change their assumptions about their own abilities, providing them with specific training in decision making and conflict management, and giving them steady doses of encouragement.

Consider Julie, a dedicated employee in our company's call center. A natural leader, she loathed the idea of being one. Though she was an able, intelligent, and compassionate team player, Julie simply didn't believe she had the right to make decisions for others. Moreover, she had worked for too many bosses who routinely took credit for her work. She had convinced herself that being a boss meant being nasty and that altering her style to fit such a mold was neither possible nor appealing. Yet because she was both nurturing and competent, her coworkers naturally turned to her for guidance and feedback. In fact, Julie was already their informal leader. When her manager asked Julie to apply for the job of call center leader and for the leadership development program, Julie reluctantly applied and was accepted to the program. Yet she continued to see herself not as a leader but as a team member who had some additional administrative duties.

It was soon clear that Julie would need to do more than be just another team member. Julie's new team of 15 call-center associates—many of whom were rumored to have been "dumped" in her area by managers who couldn't motivate them or fire them—had a reputation for consistently failing to meet quality and productivity objectives. But still Julie maintained a low profile; faced with decisions, she demurred. A comment she made in a one-on-one coaching session captured her attitude perfectly: "Who am I to make these decisions? I'm not more important than the people I work with. I'll let them decide. They are adults."

In learning to become a good manager, Julie first needed to change her negative assumptions about leadership. In her case, 360-degree feedback was an excellent tool. She scored high in her ability to handle customer problems, get results, and collaborate with peers to solve problems. And people loved her; she received kudos for

creating a work environment that was fun and for helping people maintain perspective, even when call volumes
peaked. One person wrote: "I would follow Julie wherever
she went." Still, criticism followed praise: "I only wish she
had enough confidence in her ability to just make decisions and take the lead." Julie was taken aback by the
comments: She realized that she was already the empathetic leader she herself had craved, but she also learned
that she was a long way from reaching her potential.
Sharing the feedback she'd received with her team, Julie
explained why she had been reluctant to make decisions.
She then solicited the group's expectations of her and
outlined her aspirations for them.

To help Julie become more comfortable making decisions and managing conflicts, a mentor created a series
of hypothetical problems for her to handle. During
coaching sessions, we asked Julie to make and justify
decisions about everyday call-center dilemmas. A sample
problem went something like this: "A customer calls to
complain because he hasn't received the money he
requested be withdrawn from his account. You discover
that the money was mistakenly wired to another customer's account. The amount is significant, and your
boss has been encouraging everyone to find a way to
serve the customer without losing money. Do you send
the money back to the caller with an apology immediately, or do you try to get the money back from the other
customer first?" Julie had to ask herself, "Which has a
worse effect on Nationwide's bottom line—the cost of
the reimbursement or the cost of going through a collection agency to try to recover the funds?" She chose to
reimburse the customer—and when her mentor told her
that he would have made the same decision, she felt
affirmed in her judgment. The mentor added that it costs

Nationwide more to bring in a new customer than to keep an existing one, so you want to nurture those relationships. As Julie became practiced at thinking through managerial decisions in a safe environment, she gradually learned to trust her own thought processes, knowledge of the business, and ability to make good decisions on the spot.

Teaching Julie to manage conflict required a more forceful combination of coaching and hands-on experience. In one instance, an employee felt that a colleague wasn't carrying his weight. Resentful, the employee refused to take up the slack on days when her coworker was away from the office, which placed an additional burden on the other team members. In the past, Julie would not have tried to interfere, simply hoping that the disagreeing parties would sort things out by themselves. But during coaching, she came to understand that such infighting would seriously compromise her department's productivity. She learned how to smooth conflicts by listening to the two opposing sides, then demanding that the combatants focus on their work instead of each other. As part of her development, she was also required to meet with each associate on her team to discuss career goals and progress—including the sensitive subject of performance improvement, a challenge for any risk-averse manager.

Critical to Julie's transformation was an enormous amount of encouragement. During the entire development process, coaches, colleagues, bosses, and mentors were all called upon to provide her with constant, encouraging feedback. The more frequently Julie heard that she had made a good decision or had handled a conflict well, the more confident she became.

More than likely, Julie will never be overly confident, but she has learned to take a stand when necessary and to manage around her self-doubt. The team has responded by exceeding every production measure. Her natural ability to rally others won over even the most skeptical and unmotivated associates, and quality scores rose as the individuals began working as a cohesive team. Just three months after holding the expectations meeting, Julie's team doubled its productivity, lowered its absenteeism, and earned the division's top ranking for quality.

The Arrogant Leader

Only 10% of our participants fall into this category, but they stand out the most because they can be brazen. Arrogant leaders are just as insecure as reluctant ones, but they overcompensate for their self-doubt by convincing themselves that they are already terrific managers. Because they are ambitious self-marketers, most organizations promote them without a second thought. Yet arrogant leaders can wreak havoc on their teams. Transforming such people into capable managers requires a rude awakening in the form of harsh feedback, hands-on practice in empathetic listening and teamwork, and even threats of demotion or dismissal.

Steve, for example, was an extremely competitive and technically competent customer-service team leader who had already been promoted to manager on the strength of his individual performance. Talented at handling difficult customers, Steve's belief in his own capabilities had been reinforced by several promotions from an entry-level position. During our first coaching session, Steve displayed overweening confidence, saying he knew he could do "any management job." In further sessions, we talked about the ways arrogance and ambition can bump a career off track, but he didn't take the hint. Rather, he noted that he'd never recommend one of his own arrogant team members for promotion. When we suggested he might have a similar attitude, he took offense, saying: "Ask anyone I work with. They love working with me. They know I am bored in this job and could do more."

Steve's confrontation with his mistaken self-image began during his 360-degree feedback session, in which he had rated himself as perfect in all categories. The feedback from others was, predictably, the opposite. Scoring low in nearly all areas and hearing that he was considered self-serving came as the first of many shocks.

Clinging to the false image of his own perfection, Steve was slower to make progress than other program participants. Like many arrogant leaders, Steve spent a lot of time laying the groundwork for his next job—scheduling numerous lunches and meetings with executives in other areas of the company—at the expense of his current one. He excused his lack of interaction with his team by saying he trusted his people. But as his team's performance began to suffer, Steve went so far as to ask one of his direct reports to exaggerate the team's production numbers.

This ethical lapse and the attendant humiliation were blessings in disguise, for they provided the breakthrough Steve needed to correct his behavior. A written warning was placed in his file. He was notified that if he didn't turn his performance around, or if he demonstrated any further lapses in judgment, he risked getting fired. During the hard-line coaching session that followed, we pointed out to Steve that his behavior, not that of his team, had led to his current situation, and he needed to take responsibility for it. Steve's self-deceptive armor finally cracked. For the first time, he admitted his fear that people would find out the truth about him—that he was unsure of himself and had no idea how to improve team performance. Steve's manager also took a hand in deconstructing Steve's lifelong assumption that being a leader meant looking good. He told Steve, "You're talented, but you're not fooling anyone. If your behavior doesn't improve, I will never recommend you for promotion, and you may end up being fired."

The next step in Steve's metamorphosis was a forced walk in his associates' shoes. One aspect of his development plan focused on trading places with his direct reports. They were to teach him about managing the workflow, as well as about their other responsibilities and concerns. The more he proved himself able to learn from others, the more successful he would be. This hurdle was huge, for Steve's past actions had cost him the team's trust. At first, associates were reluctant to share ideas, complaints, or anything at all with him.

But as people witnessed Steve's sincere effort to change, heard his thoughtful questions, and saw him listening carefully to their answers, they began to forgive him. A self-deprecating honesty began to replace Steve's phony self-confidence. Because he finally understood that his own success depended on that of his team, he was able to laugh at himself. After graduating from the program, he continued to work extremely hard to change his arrogant habits. Though he's not perfect, Steve is now one of our best mentors—in part because he understands the value of tough love.

The Unknown Leader

Roughly 25% of our program participants are "unknown leaders"—ambitious, highly competent, yet cautious people who form relationships more slowly and

tentatively than others. Because they are often introverted, their personal networks are small and they rarely
initiate conversations. People don't usually look to them
for leadership, and they have little "brand recognition" in
their organizations.

To transform unknown leaders into effective managers again requires 360-degree feedback, followed by
careful deconstruction of their underlying belief that
networking means glad-handing, and that it is a waste of
time. It's also effective to force unknown leaders into
meetings with new people, but, as is the case with reluctant leaders, this requires a lot of monitoring and support. Additionally, we've found hands-on management
experience in an unfamiliar environment to be helpful in
bringing unknown leaders out of their shells.

A commissions analyst named John personified the
unknown leader. Though he excelled at financial analysis, customer service, and problem solving, John was not
one for small talk; his entire focus was on achieving his
own results. His fast pace made him seem too busy to
entertain questions. He smiled rarely and walked the
halls with his head down. His demeanor caused some to
conclude he was unapproachable or aloof. Repeatedly
passed over for promotion, John was beginning to feel
resentful.

His manager noted John's grumblings and suggested
he enroll in the leadership development program. The
initial 360-degree feedback session was telling. John
received average scores and no comments from his peers,
simply because no one knew much about him. During
the coaching sessions that followed, we asked John how
he expected to climb the corporate ladder if nobody
knew who he was. Then we discussed his underlying
assumptions. To John, quality work spoke for itself. Net-

working was phony, something that people with less talent had to pursue in order to get noticed. In his view, a relationship was worth having only if the other party shared common ground with him and was capable of a deep conversation. We proposed to John that his assumption that hard work alone merited promotion was outdated. To get ahead, he needed to think of himself as product in need of a brand. Like products in the marketplace, we explained, people are associated with certain characteristics: Joe is brilliant with customers; Jane is creative and innovative; Bill is a master with numbers.

John remained somewhat cynical about being compared to a little-known product, but he saw the point. He responded well to our stark questions: "What have you been doing to move your career forward? Has that been working for you? Why not? What else could you do?" Understanding that he would not get promoted if he didn't begin to network, he decided to try to change. But changing was hard. John couldn't simply flip a switch and become a sociable person. First, he needed to become more comfortable meeting and talking with new people. To this end, we required him to do what Steve had always done as a matter of course—regularly invite more senior managers to lunch. We also required John to interview his own prospective mentors.

We prepared John for these interview sessions by giving him a list of questions—"Tell me about your business?" "What was your career path?" "What do you look for when you're hiring a manager?" and so on—that we also sent to the interviewees. John was surprised to discover that he could hold serious, interesting conversations with total strangers. Like Julie, he learned that he didn't have to totally change his style. In fact, he learned that his natural ability to think analytically and drive to a deeper level in conversations impressed others. And again like Julie, John needed ongoing encouragement, so we made sure that he heard the interviewees' positive comments about him. As these meetings became more habitual for John, he began to look forward to them. In time, he became more approachable, and as a result, his relationships with his coworkers deepened. John began to see that networking was about building authentic relationships.

Another way to bring unknown leaders out of their shells is to give them unfamiliar assignments in new environments. This forces them into close contact with other people—and out of their sphere of technical expertise. This was the case with John. He knew little about the life insurance division he was assigned to take over for a manager on temporary medical leave and was understandably apprehensive. Still, he took the opportunity to build his brand by coaching people, running meetings, overseeing projects, and dealing with problems. Early in this new role, John quickly helped the team deal with a tough customer complaint, prompting his peers to talk about his contribution and good attitude. Eventually, a buzz developed around John—and today, he's considered a top candidate for future management roles.

The Workaholic

By far the largest number of managers in our program— fully 45%—are workaholics. Many have anxiety-driven, addictive personalities, choosing work over and above family, spiritual growth, sports, hobbies, love, or friendship. Of course, workaholism has degrees of severity:

There are those people who love their jobs and work long hours without suffering negative consequences. But acute workaholics are like hamsters on a wheel, laboring relentlessly to finish endless daily tasks. Typically extroverts hooked on activity and action, severe workaholics are far more likely to suffer from burnout, stress, and the attendant physical problems—chronic fatigue, heart disease, high blood pressure, and so on. Unfortunately, most companies continue to reward workaholism.

Our own informal research has confirmed that employees respond far more favorably to well-rounded managers with outside interests. They willingly work harder for such managers because they know that when the team is reaching its goals, their personal lives will be respected as well. Our challenge with workaholics, then, is to demonstrate that their modus operandi of working harder rather than smarter is a zero-sum game. Rather than rewarding workaholism, we try to punish it.

Mark, for example, was a classic workaholic. In his first job out of college, he worked 100 hours a week, and his company rewarded him with a string of raises and promotions. By the time Mark's organization was acquired by Nationwide and he came into the leadership development program, he had been a systems project manager for seven years with a track record of positive results. But he had never worked less than 90 hours a week.

During our first coaching session, Mark expressed frustration with some incorrect billing statements issued six weeks earlier. His colleagues didn't take work seriously, he said. He'd lost touch with friends. He blamed his steep weight gain on scant time for exercise. Six-week-old billing issues were his life. Deep down, Mark distrusted everyone. If making up for others' perceived irresponsibility was what was required for his own career advancement, well then, work was his life.

Because workaholics tend to focus on objective measures, 360-degree feedback is not usually an effective training tool for this type of leader. Where participants like Julie, Steve, and John saw areas where they needed to improve, the feedback merely reinforced Mark's belief that he was doing just fine by any objective measure— belying the spiritual, emotional, and physical sacrifices he'd made to become what he sadly was. So we tried another assessment model—the wheel-shaped "healthy leader" model borrowed from professional development consultant Lewis R. Timberlake, which describes the ideal manager as one who is strong in physical, emotional, spiritual, business, family, and social skills. This holistic model proved much more powerful. Having observed that he'd failed in four of the six categories, Mark responded to the kind of wake-up call Scrooge faced: What will people say about you at your funeral?

During the weeks that followed, Mark considered how he'd lost friends, happiness, perspective, and health. With his manager's help, Mark devised a development plan that required him to balance, on a weekly basis, his personal life and work demands. In particular, he was to leave work before 7 PM every day. When Mark wasn't originally able to meet the goal, his manager suggested that working late might cost him consideration for future promotions. The suggestion was clearly absurd to Mark, but he was forced him to ask himself, "Is working so hard really worth risking my job?"

At first, Mark made an awkward attempt to delegate to others. Unaccustomed to the additional work, his associates submitted hurried and incomplete assignments—convincing Mark he'd been right all along. But rather than doing the work himself, Mark chose to talk to his team about his predicament and his attempt to "get a life," to which one team member responded, "Thank goodness. You're too young to be so old and grumpy."

Everyone chipped in to help Mark get his life back. They pushed him out the door before 7. They made certain he reconnected with old college buddies and played golf with them. During these golf outings, Mark's curiosity, creativity, and sense of humor rebounded. At work, he began chatting with coworkers about Ohio State football games and joking around. He started sharing more about himself and taking a genuine interest in people. He also started taking the team to lunch occasionally. He soon found he was better able to set priorities for himself and his staff members; they responded with their own ideas and redoubled energy. Not long after, Mark the golfer and Mark the football fan became Mark the well-rounded senior manager.

IN THE PROCESS OF WORKING WITH the four types of managers, we've learned something about the efficacy of the various development methods we apply. We believe that had we not developed a tailored approach, we would be setting up our managers for failure. While one type of person responds very well to one form of "treatment," the same approach backfires with someone else. Reluctant and unknown leaders require extra doses of support and encouragement, while the threat of harsh consequences makes all the difference with arrogant leaders and workaholics.

Today, we're expanding our leadership development program to the entire company; our goal is eventually to work with all managers in the organization. We have created a process that is turning out leaders that understand how to engage employees, no matter what position they hold in the company, to accomplish great things. Nationwide's culture is becoming one that nurtures talented managers, rather than one that leaves them to struggle through a Darwinian survival game.

Originally published in March 2003
Reprint R0303H

No Ordinary Boot Camp

NOEL M. TICHY

Executive Summary

MANY COMPANIES NOW RUN boot camps—comprehensive orientation programs designed to help new hires
hit the ground running. They're intense and intimidating,
and new employees emerge from them with strong
bonds to other recruits and to the organization. But at
Trilogy, organizational consultant Noel Tichy discovered
one program that's a breed apart.

In this article, Tichy gives us a detailed tour of Trilogy's boot camp, Trilogy University, to demonstrate why
it's so different—and so effective. Like the best boot
camps, it serves as an immersion in both the technical
skills new recruits will need for their jobs and Trilogy's
corporate culture, which emphasizes risk-taking, teamwork, humility, and a strong customer focus. But this is a
new-employee orientation session that's so fundamental
to the company as a whole that it's presided over by the

CEO and top corporate executives for fully six months of the year.

Why? In two three-month sessions, these top executives hone their own strategic thinking about the company as they decide what to teach the new recruits each session. They also find the company's next generation of new products as they judge the innovative ideas the recruits are tasked with developing—making the program Trilogy's main R&D engine. And they pull the company's rising technical stars into mentoring roles for the new recruits, helping to build the next generation of top leadership.

After spending months on-site studying Trilogy University, Tichy came away highly impressed by the power of the virtuous teaching cycle the program has set in motion. Leaders of the organization are learning from recruits at the same time that the recruits are learning from the leaders. It's a model, he argues, that other companies would do well to emulate.

CORPORATE BOOT CAMPS. We've all heard about them. Many of us have lived through them. In my case, I've even invented a number of them. It's fair to say that, while some achieve their goals better than others, they're all pretty much the same. They typically focus on knowledge transfer—informing new hires, for instance, about the company's products and markets and how to access key resources in the organization. The best ones, like those at GE and Ford, do this by having the recruits work on real business problems, where intense teamwork is required to meet tight deadlines (a technique I've described elsewhere as "compressed action learning"). I've studied them all. I thought I'd seen it all.

But then I saw Trilogy University. It was 1998, and I was traveling around the country, studying corporate universities as part of a benchmarking research project on action learning. Within days of my arrival, I knew Trilogy University was a breed apart—in fact, my definition of best practice shot out to the horizon line. I've spent hundreds of hours since then at TU, documenting its unconventional approach—and its phenomenal results. (It should be stated, by way of full disclosure, that I briefly consulted to Trilogy last year on the matter of its reorganization. But my relationship to the company and its university at this point is purely as an observer.)

Modeled after Marine Corps basic training, a corporate boot camp is designed to push new recruits to their limits. Each day offers some nearly insurmountable challenge, and the reward for overcoming it is an even harder one the next day. It's intense and intimidating, but people emerge on the other end of the program highly confident that they are prepared for anything. They also come away with deep bonds to their fellow recruits and strong ties to the organization.

Those two goals—preparedness and bonding—are usually the whole focus of a boot camp, and achieving them is worth a great deal. That's why so many of the top-performing companies put their faith in such programs. In the mid-1980s, I ran General Electric's Crotonville leadership development center, where I led the development of its Corporate Entry Leadership Conference, a three-day program in which new hires learn about GE's strategy, its culture, and a bit about themselves. "Old man Watson" at IBM ran them, as did Ross Perot when he founded EDS, as does Andy Grove at Intel. And for years, the commercial banks have run their commercial-lending boot camps for college hires. In the past decade, consulting firms and service organizations have dramatically increased their investments in boot camps for new recruits. Accounting giant Arthur Andersen, for instance, has a 700-bed facility in St. Charles, Illinois, which runs at capacity year-round. Many old-line industrials have also set them up because they realize that energizing new hires and engaging them in the culture is just as critical as making sure they have the technical skills to do their specific jobs.

The interesting thing about Trilogy University is that it achieves those goals and more. Much more. It also serves as the company's primary R&D engine and as its way of developing its next generation of leadership. It even succeeds as the impetus and incubator for Trilogy's strategic thinking. How can it do all that? By now, it almost couldn't fail to, thanks to a virtuous cycle that was established early and continues to gain momentum. In the simplest terms, these things happen at TU because top leadership is on the scene and deeply engaged in it—and top leadership stays on the scene and deeply engaged in TU because these essential activities are happening there.

Welcome to Trilogy

Trilogy University is the orientation program of Austin, Texas-based Trilogy, designed to turn the company's raw recruits—hired straight off the campuses of MIT, Stanford, U. Michigan, and the like—into highly productive contributors. Started in 1995, it is the brainchild of Trilogy's president and CEO, Joe Liemandt, and its vice president of marketing, John Price.

The company has a pressing need for new-employee orientation because its growth has been extremely rapid, and the biggest drag on growth has been the difficulty of recruiting and bringing new talent up to speed. Trilogy started fast out of the gate in 1989 when Liemandt nailed a market opportunity to create "configuration software" for large manufacturers like Hewlett-Packard and Boeing. The products these companies sell have innumerable variants, as alternative components are assembled to suit each buyer's highly specific preferences. Trilogy's software solves a huge problem traditionally faced in the selling process by allowing a salesperson with a laptop to translate a customer's needs into a workable specification. The software spots where components are incompatible, for instance, or where one part requires another, and it configures a system that will work. Then—and this is really important to those salespeople—it produces an accurate price quote on the spot.

Trilogy's breakthrough allowed it to do something most small software companies only dream of: sign up brand-name accounts like Hewlett-Packard while the product was still in its infancy. Since then, Trilogy has expanded on its original offering to launch e-commerce applications for both the buying and selling of products, and its revenues have grown to about $200 million. Along the way, its employee base has grown 35% annually. In 2000, the company brought 450 new hires into an existing organization of 1,000.

Joe Liemandt realized early on that, as each influx of new hires came through the doors, the company needed to equip them with not only the skills required for their jobs but also the vision and values with which they should align their work. But because each new group represented a fair proportion of the whole organization, assimilation wasn't going to happen in some natural, organic way. It would have to be deliberately managed.

Having to compress a great deal of learning and acculturation into a short time frame, Liemandt decided he needed a boot camp.

Three High-Pressure Months

"The first day, Joe walks in. And, like, his very few first words are, 'You're going to be the future of Trilogy—the company is relying on you—and everybody's waiting on you.'"

The speaker is Vince Mallet, a computer science master's grad who was wearing a Java T-shirt, his long hair in a neat ponytail, and a broad grin as he recently gave me the student's view of TU. Liemandt's message was apparently hitting home. Mallet told me, "I just want to go out in the company and be able to have that impact." It would be a tough several weeks before he got that chance.

Trilogy University is run twice a year. In the summer, it currently includes 170 to 200 hires, and in the winter about 60, all coming straight from campus. A class typically has a sprinkling of freshly minted master's and PhDs, and a fair number of liberal arts majors, but it's mostly drawn from undergraduate computer science departments. The program generally lasts 12 weeks. It's structured to take students through a well-thought-out process to develop skills, relationships, and values, which they then apply in intense R&D projects before they're ultimately introduced as a positive new force into the rest of the organization.

MONTH ONE

When you arrive at Trilogy University, you are assigned to a section and to an instruction track. Your section, a group of about 20, is your social group for the duration of TU. You share a section leader (an experienced person from Trilogy who serves as a mentor) and virtually all of your time with these people. Tracks are designed to be microcosms of future work life at Trilogy. For example, as a future developer or consultant, you might learn about technologies like XML and JSP one week by building a customizable sales analysis Web site for a fictional company. The technical challenges in such exercises closely mimic real customer engagements, but the time frames are dramatically compressed. The assignments pile up week after week for the first month, each one successively more challenging than the last.

During that time, you're being constantly measured and evaluated, as assignment grades and comments are entered into a database monitoring your progress. The functional training is so intense it would be easy to assume that it is the most important goal of TU. But Allan Drummond, the Trilogy vice president who runs TU, says that's not the case. "If people don't learn Java in TU, I don't care. They're very bright—they can pick up what they need. But if they don't develop nearly unbreakable bonds with fellow TUers, if they don't learn to prioritize and make smart decisions, if they don't leave charged up, then TU is a failure."

The goals Drummond is emphasizing are the focus of the sections. Unlike tracks, sections continue past the first month. In a sense, they last for life. Effectiveness at Trilogy depends on having trusting relationships with coworkers, and sections are designed to prime that process. That's why Vince Mallet explained to me, "on the second day, we were all asked to tell the most significant emotional experience of our lives." Vince says some of the students' first reactions were cynical: "Yeah, we're going to tell stories about us. Whatever." But the technique worked its magic as people began to talk and listen. Before long, he says, "some people were crying; some people were making other people cry. And I thought, whoa—this is totally unusual." People were getting deeply acquainted, not incidentally but intentionally. The individuals in each section represent a cross section of functions; upon graduation from TU, the students will disperse to all corners of Trilogy, and the trust and bonds they develop will form horizontal networks linking them to people throughout the company for the rest of their careers.

Beyond developing skills and relationships, month one of Trilogy University also begins to instill values. Humility is one of the values Liemandt wants to see, and that's one reason the tracks deliberately stretch students beyond the point of failure. Other values are introduced through what people at Trilogy refer to as "big talks," which Liemandt or other Trilogy stars have with the whole TU class, usually in a Socratic style, and which are further discussed and debated in sections. Students learn early that Trilogy values creativity, innovation, and being a force for positive change in the workplace. They learn that Trilogy wants to see teamwork and a strong belief that success means solving the customer's problem. More than anything, they learn that Trilogy values risk taking. Along with the skills and relationships forged in month one, these values will be sorely tested in month two.

MONTH TWO

Month two is TU project month. This is when the TUers, most of them 22 years old and employees for all of a month, take on the responsibility of inventing the company's future. "We tell them that, in order for the company to survive, they have to come up with a frame-breaking great new business idea," says Liemandt. "And they believe it because I really believe it."

Liemandt's learned, he says, "the hard way" that taking risks and suffering the consequences is a crucial part of any business. When he decided to launch Trilogy, he was in his senior year at Stanford. Rather than miss what might be a narrow window of opportunity, he decided to drop out and dedicate himself full-time to it. At least one very accomplished businessman, a former GE senior executive (who also happened to be his father), told him: "You're a moron."

The TU project is Liemandt's way of giving new recruits his own experience all over again. In teams of three to five people, they have to come up with an idea, create a business model for it, build the product, and develop the marketing plan. In trying to launch bold new ideas in a hyperaccelerated time frame, they gain a deep appreciation of the need to set priorities, evaluate probabilities, and measure results. Mind you, these projects are not hypothetical—they're the real thing. But even more important, when each team presents its innovation, Liemandt is there, deciding whether or not to put up the money to launch it. It's exhausting but it's also energizing, because Trilogy's best and most senior people are in the mix. New employees know they're getting noticed and that their ideas have a chance of being taken up.

How big is that chance? About 15% of the projects survive beyond the month that's allocated to them in TU. It's that humility thing again. Drummond describes the reaction of recruits who think their ideas are brilliant but then see them fail. "They're like, 'We stink. Not near good enough.' Actually, we never want that feeling to end. Because the minute you get arrogant, someone comes and beats you."

At the same time, the seriousness with which Liemandt and all the rest of Trilogy take the projects builds confidence. "We encourage them to go for the fence with their ideas and, while we don't reward failure around here, we don't punish them for it either," says Liemandt. "So, when people leave TU, most of them are thinking, 'I know I can make a difference, and I am not afraid to try'—which is exactly what we want them to think."

MONTH THREE

Month three at Trilogy University is all about finding your place and having a broader impact in the larger organization. A few students continue with their TU projects, but most move on to "graduation projects," which generally are assignments within the various Trilogy business units. People leave TU on a rolling basis as they find sponsors out in the company who are willing to take them on.

The graduation process is a meeting between the graduate, the new manager, and the section leader. Before the meeting, each has been asked to evaluate the TUer on his or her various abilities. At the meeting, the three of them discuss the evaluation to resolve disagreements. "We don't just want understanding; we want agreement," Drummond says. "On all of the rankings where there is a disparity, they have to reach an agreement." The TUers have also written lists of objectives and their thoughts on how they want their careers to unfold. The manager responds to these with a list of specific goals that the TUer must agree to. Typically, the manager will set three to five yearlong goals that include a skill development goal, a mainline execution goal, and an organizational development goal. In addition, the manager creates another plan focused on creating the job assignments and coaching opportunities that will help the TUer reach his or her longer-term career goals.

"We want everyone here to be a star. We won't graduate TUers until they have found positions they want and where the new manager will take responsibility for helping them become a star," explains former TU head Danielle Rios. The TU faculty sometimes help persuade managers who are reluctant to take a risk, but a TUer who ultimately can't find a sponsor is out of the company.

It's the rare TU graduate who can't find a home within Trilogy because, clearly, Trilogy University succeeds at the basics of basic training. Graduates emerge from it prepared—by their skills, their relationships, and their values—to hit the ground running. But what really sets this boot camp apart from others I know is that it contributes much more to Trilogy than that. First, thanks to the energy and attention devoted to the TU projects, TU has become the company's primary research and development engine. Second, it has become the setting for Trilogy's leadership development. Third, it provides a great context and impetus for management to revisit and communicate strategic direction. And fourth, it serves as a constant source of organizational renewal and transformation.

A New-Product Pipeline

Liemandt recalls the day in 1997 when a TU project team of six kids pitched the idea for selling cars on the Internet. At the time, e-commerce was still pretty much virgin territory. EBay was not alive yet. Amazon was a start-up.

Liemandt told them their idea was one of the dumbest he had ever heard. They clearly didn't understand the automotive industry, franchise laws, and how dealers would prevent this from happening. And they were totally naïve to think people would spend that kind of money over the Internet.

The team thought Liemandt was the one who was missing something, so they decided to prove him wrong. They went ahead and developed CarOrder.com, lined up struggling dealers who were willing to cooperate, and—lo and behold—started racking up sales. Today, one of Trilogy's most talked-about businesses is its global alliance with Ford. Without the consumer-side technology, experience, and credibility Trilogy developed from that TU project—the CarOrder.com Web site won *PC Magazine*'s 2000 Editors' Choice for Best Car-Buying Site—the Ford relationship would not have happened. Liemandt, who first designed TU projects purely as a learning exercise, has come to see them as his biggest source of strategic innovation.

It makes perfect sense, if you think about it. Playing the role of the venture capitalist, Liemandt is wholly focused on the merits of the ideas as business propositions. And because he and other senior managers are paying attention, the students are truly giving their all on these projects.

Meanwhile, the intensity of the bonds between teammates helps ensure that deep collaboration is taking place among them, leading to higher creativity. And the fact that these are new hires straight out of college means their ideas are less likely to be constrained by past practices—at TU or anywhere else.

For all these reasons, R&D gets done at Trilogy and gets done well. Since 1995, TU projects have produced revenues of $25 million and have formed the basis for $100 million in new business for the company.

A recent TU class, for example, developed Fast Cycle Time, an Internet-time delivery methodology now being used by more than 20 of Trilogy's customers. In late 1999, several TUers created a Web site called IveBeenGood. com, which enabled shoppers to put products from popular retail sites like Amazon or ShopNow directly into a single shopping cart, which IveBeenGood hosted. Only nine months after its creation, a refined version of this universal shopping-cart technology, renamed Uber-Works and still run by TUers, was sold to Network Commerce for $13 million. The initial investment was $2 million.

The Next Generation of Leaders

TU also succeeds as a proving ground for developing the next generation of leadership at Trilogy. I've mentioned that the section leaders are experienced people. What I haven't said yet is that these are the best and brightest technical stars Trilogy has to offer—and that they dedicate themselves 100% to TU for three months at a time. Trilogy's chief scientist, David Franke, for example, was a section leader in 1999. So was Scott Snyder, Trilogy's vice president of development, who in summer 2000 asked for a turn as a section leader before he moved over to help grow Trilogy's European operations.

This is an extraordinary investment, to be sure. But consider the payback. In the hothouse of TU, and under the direct eye of Liemandt, these technical people are learning and testing out the essential skills they need to be effective leaders: inspiring others, mentoring talent, evaluating performance, communicating vision and strategy, and more. During their three months at TU, they are not only exposed to Liemandt's latest ideas about the direction of the company, they're also engaged with him as partners in developing and implementing those ideas. In the process, they are transformed from being members of the "old Trilogy" into dedicated change agents participating in its next round of transformation.

Again, it makes perfect sense. But what a contrast with typical practice, which assigns orientation duty to the staff the business can most easily spare or outsources it to consultants and professional trainers. At Trilogy University, believe it or not, it's an honor to be asked to instruct. Trilogians know this is the fast-track experience they need to move up in the company. A case in point is Ben Zaniello, a leading product manager in Trilogy's financial services practice, who actually declined a promotion in 2000, opting instead to become a section leader. "I felt that to really drive our financial service offerings forward into places like on-line wealth management," Zaniello says, "section leading was a better opportunity for growth and for really innovating."

Clarity on Strategy

Another benefit was at first unexpected but is now a crucial piece of TU's contribution to Trilogy's success: twice a year, Liemandt and other Trilogy leaders must decide what they want to teach and how they want to focus the new class of hires.

For any leader, regardless of whether he or she is ever in a classroom setting, having what I call a "teachable point of view" is crucial. This is essentially a clear idea about where the company (or organization or team) needs to go, a general understanding about how it's going to get there, and the ability to explain it in a way that inspires others. Leaders' TPOVs must be firm and clear, but they must also constantly evolve to take new conditions into account. What TU does for Liemandt and other Trilogy lead-ers is to compel them to update their TPOVs at least twice a year. As a result, Joe and the senior leadership are continually challenged and given candid feedback that helps them improve the way they craft and share their vision. TU is the impetus and the process for improving Liemandt and his senior people as leaders.

Organizational Transformation

There's at least one more thing TU contributes to Trilogy that a typical boot camp does not—and it may be the most important thing of all. It serves as a force for orga-nizational renewal and transformation. Traditionally, orientation programs are designed to teach newcomers to fit into the existing organization. But TU sees its fresh hires as its best chance to change the company. "With each TU class, we have the opportunity to create in the minds of 60 or 160 new people the vision of Trilogy not as it is but as we would like it to be," says Drummond. "We make sure that they bond into a strong trust net-work among themselves and with the leaders who men-tor them in TU, which gives them confidence. Then we send them out into the company, where they have the critical mass to make a real impact."

This, in fact, was the goal that led to Trilogy Univer-sity in the first place. As Liemandt tells it now, he was concerned in 1994 that the new people coming in might have their eyes on a rather short-term prize. The company was a one-trick pony; it had a very hot product, and a quick sale or an IPO could have paid off handsomely. Liemandt had already spotted that kind of perspective in some of his colleagues, and he didn't like it. He was in it for the long haul, and he wanted an organization devoted to building, as it says in the company's motto, "the next great software company." So that's when he decided to gather together a team of new hires, isolate them from the legacy organization, and spend three months helping them get the religion.

This is a big part of why the TUers' entry into the company is so carefully orchestrated. In the first few weeks of TU, they're highly isolated from the rest of the company. As the weeks go by, the amount of contact increases. By the third month, they're ready to venture out into the company, while retaining their home base and their support network back in TU.

"I and most of Trilogy don't think of TU as a training program. It is a transformational experience," Drummond says. It transforms the TUers, it transforms Liemandt and other Trilogy leaders, and, ultimately, it transforms the company.

The Virtuous Teaching Cycle

Of everything I've seen at Trilogy University, I'm most impressed with the power of the virtuous teaching cycle it has put in motion. The leaders of the organization are learning from the recruits as the recruits are learning from the leaders. Each element in place here—new-hire training, product innovation, leadership development, and the rest—fuels the others. It's not just that all these things get done at Trilogy University. It's that all of them get done better than they would otherwise.

Now stop and read that last sentence again, because it's big. *It's all done better.*

New hires learn faster because they are working on real projects, with guidance from the best managerial talent in the company and with the full knowledge that their efforts are not going unnoticed. Leaders in training learn more because they have real leadership responsibilities and must engage thoughtfully with the vision and strategy of the company. Even R&D pays off better because people with unconstrained perspectives are brainstorming ideas just as they are internalizing that vision and strategy. The commitment and personal involvement of the CEO keeps the cycle in motion. He serves as a role model for it and demands it of everyone else.

So Why Doesn't Everyone Do This?

I'll say it again for emphasis: what I have observed at Trilogy University is completely different from what I've seen in other corporate training programs—even in other boot camps. So why is that? Why didn't someone like Jack Welch think this up? For that matter, why didn't *I*?

In Jack's defense and mine, I'll point out that this revolutionary model was also an evolutionary one—and arose from a particular circumstance that few companies share. Back in 1994, Trilogy was a very small company hiring so many people at once that the incoming group had the power to make a needed shift in the culture. Under those circumstances, to claim that new-employee orientation is the best use of a CEO's time—even three months of his time—is not such a stretch. But how many places does this describe? At this point, not even Trilogy.

Happily, TU evolved by adding other elements so important to the company's future that it remains the best use of senior management's time. In fact, at this point, the cycle is so powerful it's hard to imagine it breaking down. And the evolution continues: starting in 2001, Liemandt has decided to bring customers into the process. Selected customers can sponsor a TU session, sending their own executives to the program, which would then focus on a set of their key business challenges. Trilogy will get invaluable executive exposure for its R&D efforts and its leadership development process. The customer will get several man-years of innovation time—and a potential breakthrough. The point is, this isn't a case of taking top people out of the action. This *is* the action.

The challenge for other companies, then, is to set this kind of virtuous cycle in motion given their larger scale and established processes. Most will have to overcome a lot of inertia; some will even have to reverse a cycle that's going in the opposite direction.

That's not an easy task, and along the way the most dedicated reformer will constantly run up against some predictable objections: It's too expensive. We can't take our best people off the line. We can't leave innovation up to kids. We can't trust them not to train on our dime, then take their skills elsewhere. Excuses, excuses.

I'm not saying there aren't legitimate reasons that a full-blown TU-style boot camp might not be for you. Maybe most of your new hires don't come straight from campus and simply can't deal with the intense work-life imbalance of a boot camp. Maybe you're not in a hot enough business—like pre-IPO software—to attract the kind of talent that could dream up your next big hit (although Liemandt would certainly counter that the best way to attract talent is to offer this kind of opportunity). There may be more reasons that TU can't be replicated everywhere. But it seems clear that many other companies can do this—and could reap the same results. What has held the rest of us back, I hope, is not that we couldn't use this model but that we have not yet imagined it, and we have not yet seen it succeed.

We've discovered it now, and it seems to work. Now it's up to other leaders to imagine it in their own organizations. More than anything, making it succeed will require top management on the scene, truly committed to learning as a two-way street. Without those people and that attitude, no orientation program will get much respect or have much impact. With them, the impact can go far, *far* beyond the goals of simple orientation. That's what has happened at Trilogy.

Trilogy University Goes Virtual

ONE PARTICULAR INNOVATION coming out of Trilogy University strikes me as a perfect encapsulation of all that goes on there. It's a software application called Leadership.com, conceived by a TU project team in the winter of 1999.

That team, freshly inspired by CEO Joe Liemandt's vision and energy, decided the word wasn't getting out far enough. It was great to have Joe presenting his most current point of view to the newest hires, but wouldn't the impact be greater if the whole organization could be hearing it too? With that in mind, they developed an Internet platform for Liemandt to post his "teachable point of view" and get feedback. That quickly expanded into Leadership.com, a multimedia platform for sharing, responding to, and holding discussions about ideas. Moreover, it isn't just Joe broadcasting those ideas. At this point, more than 200 Trilogians have posted video clips in which they offer their own takes on the vision, values, and goals of the company, their business unit, their department, or just themselves. Every individual coming out of Trilogy University can now be seen on Leadership.com explaining what they think the company is all about and how they are going to help it. It's a requirement for graduation.

What's really powerful about Leadership.com, though, are the feedback people get and the thinking inspired by the exchange. Accompanying each video is a bulleted outline of its main points. There are mechanisms for viewers to numerically evaluate each presentation for both delivery and content, public forums where anyone in the company can discuss the issues raised—or not raised—in the presentations, and scorecards that show up-to-the-minute voting results. The system causes people at all levels to engage with the strategy of the company and brings TU's virtuous teaching cycle out to the broader organization.

Trilogy has been so well served by Leadership.com that it decided recently to turn it into a product for sale to others. Early customers include Percepta, Ford's joint venture in customer relationship management with TeleTech. I'm hoping it will be just the first of a potent new type of Internet tool—an "L2L" (for leader-to-leader) application.

So, consider: a group of new hires hits the ground running and creates a successful product innovation—one that helps develop leadership talent and serves as a force for positive change in the organization. Could this have happened anywhere but at Trilogy University?

Originally published in April 2001
Reprint R0104C

Teaching Smart People How to Learn

CHRIS ARGYRIS

Executive Summary

BEFORE A COMPANY CAN BECOME a learning organization, it must first resolve a learning dilemma: competitive success increasingly depends on learning, but most people don't know how to learn. What's more, those members of the organization whom many assume to be the best at learning—professionals who occupy key leadership positions—are, in fact, not very good at it.

In this article, Harvard Business School professor Chris Argyris looks at human behavior patterns that block learning in organizations, explains why well-educated professionals are prone to these patterns, and tells how companies can improve the ability of their managers and employees to learn.

Effective learning is not a matter of the right attitudes or motivation. Rather, it is the product of the way people reason about their own behavior. When asked to examine their own role in an organization's problems, most people become defensive. They put the "blame" on someone else. The defensive reasoning keeps people from examining critically the way they contribute to the very problems they are committed to solving.

The solution: companies need to make the ways managers and employees reason about their behavior a key focus of organizational learning and continuous improvement programs. Teaching people how to reason about their behavior in new and more effective ways breaks down the defenses that block organizational learning.

Any company that aspires to succeed in the tougher business environment of the 1990s must first resolve a basic dilemma: success in the marketplace increasingly depends on learning, yet most people don't know how to learn. What's more, those members of the organization that many assume to be the best at learning are, in fact, not very good at it. I am talking about the well-educated, high-powered, high-commitment professionals who occupy key leadership positions in the modern corporation.

Most companies not only have tremendous difficulty addressing this learning dilemma; they aren't even aware that it exists. The reason: they misunderstand what learning is and how to bring it about. As a result, they tend to make two mistakes in their efforts to become a learning organization.

First, most people define learning too narrowly as mere "problem solving," so they focus on identifying and correcting errors in the external environment. Solving problems is important. But if learning is to persist, managers and employees must also look inward. They need to reflect critically on their own behavior, identify the ways they often inadvertently contribute to the organization's problems, and then change how they act. In particular, they must learn how the very way they go about defining and solving problems can be a source of problems in its own right.

I have coined the terms "single loop" and "double loop" learning to capture this crucial distinction. To give a simple analogy: a thermostat that automatically turns on the heat whenever the temperature in a room drops below 68 degrees is a good example of single-loop learning. A thermostat that could ask, "Why am I set at 68 degrees?" and then explore whether or not some other temperature might more economically achieve the goal of heating the room would be engaging in double-loop learning.

Highly skilled professionals are frequently very good at single-loop learning. After all, they have spent much of their lives acquiring academic credentials, mastering one or a number of intellectual disciplines, and applying those disciplines to solve real-world problems. But ironically, this very fact helps explain why professionals are often so bad at double-loop learning.

Put simply, because many professionals are almost always successful at what they do, they rarely experience failure. And because they have rarely failed, they have never learned how to learn from failure. So whenever their single-loop learning strategies go wrong, they become defensive, screen out criticism, and put the "blame" on anyone and everyone but themselves. In short, their ability to learn shuts down precisely at the moment they need it the most.

The propensity among professionals to behave defensively helps shed light on the second mistake that companies make about learning. The common assumption is that getting people to learn is largely a matter of motivation. When people have the right attitudes and commitment, learning automatically follows. So companies focus on creating new organizational structures—compensation programs, performance reviews, corporate cultures, and the like—that are designed to create motivated and committed employees.

But effective double-loop learning is not simply a function of how people feel. It is a reflection of how they think—that is, the cognitive rules or reasoning they use to design and implement their actions. Think of these rules as a kind of "master program" stored in the brain, governing all behavior. Defensive reasoning can block learning even when the individual commitment to it is high, just as a computer program with hidden bugs can produce results exactly the opposite of what its designers had planned.

Companies can learn how to resolve the learning dilemma. What it takes is to make the ways managers and employees reason about their behavior a focus of organizational learning and continuous improvement programs. Teaching people how to reason about their behavior in new and more effective ways breaks down the defenses that block learning.

All of the examples that follow involve a particular kind of professional: fast-track consultants at major management consulting companies. But the implications of my argument go far beyond this specific occupational group. The fact is, more and more jobs—no matter what the title—are taking on the contours of "knowledge work." People at all levels of the organization must combine the mastery of some highly specialized technical expertise with the ability to work effectively in teams, form productive relationships with clients and customers, and critically reflect on and then change their own organizational practices. And the nuts and bolts of management—whether of high-powered consultants or service representatives, senior managers or factory technicians—increasingly consists of guiding and integrating the autonomous but interconnected work of highly skilled people.

How Professionals Avoid Learning

For 15 years, I have been conducting in-depth studies of management consultants. I decided to study consultants for a few simple reasons. First, they are the epitome of the highly educated professionals who play an increasingly central role in all organizations. Almost all of the consultants I've studied have MBAs from the top three or four U.S. business schools. They are also highly committed to their work. For instance, at one company, more than 90% of the consultants responded in a survey that they were "highly satisfied" with their jobs and with the company.

I also assumed that such professional consultants would be good at learning. After all, the essence of their job is to teach others how to do things differently. I found, however, that these consultants embodied the learning dilemma. The most enthusiastic about continuous improvement in their own organizations, they were also often the biggest obstacle to its complete success.

As long as efforts at learning and change focused on external organizational factors—job redesign, compensation programs, performance reviews, and leadership training—the professionals were enthusiastic participants. Indeed, creating new systems and structures was precisely the kind of challenge that well-educated, highly motivated professionals thrived on.

And yet the moment the quest for continuous improvement turned to the professionals' *own* performance, something went wrong. It wasn't a matter of bad attitude. The professionals' commitment to excellence was genuine, and the vision of the company was clear. Nevertheless, continuous improvement did not persist. And the longer the continuous improvement efforts continued, the greater the likelihood that they would produce ever-diminishing returns.

What happened? The professionals began to feel embarrassed. They were threatened by the prospect of critically examining their own role in the organization. Indeed, because they were so well paid (and generally believed that their employers were supportive and fair), the idea that their performance might not be at its best made them feel guilty.

Far from being a catalyst for real change, such feelings caused most to react defensively. They projected the blame for any problems away from themselves and onto what they said were unclear goals, insensitive and unfair leaders, and stupid clients.

Consider this example. At a premier management consulting company, the manager of a case team called a meeting to examine the team's performance on a recent consulting project. The client was largely satisfied and had given the team relatively high marks, but the manager believed the team had not created the value added that it was capable of and that the consulting company had promised. In the spirit of continuous improvement, he felt that the team could do better. Indeed, so did some of the team members.

The manager knew how difficult it was for people to reflect critically on their own work performance, especially in the presence of their manager, so he took a number of steps to make possible a frank and open discussion. He invited to the meeting an outside consultant whom team members knew and trusted—"just to keep me honest," he said. He also agreed to have the entire meeting tape-recorded. That way, any subsequent confusions or disagreements about what went on at the meeting could be checked against the transcript. Finally, the manager opened the meeting by emphasizing that no subject was off limits—including his own behavior.

"I realize that you may believe you cannot confront me," the manager said. "But I encourage you to challenge me. You have a responsibility to tell me where you think the leadership made mistakes, just as I have the responsibility to identify any I believe you made. And all of us must acknowledge our own mistakes. If we do not have an open dialogue, we will not learn."

The professionals took the manager up on the first half of his invitation but quietly ignored the second. When asked to pinpoint the key problems in the experience with the client, they looked entirely outside themselves. The clients were uncooperative and arrogant. "They didn't think we could help them." The team's own managers were unavailable and poorly prepared. "At times, our managers were not up to speed before they walked into the client meetings." In effect, the professionals asserted that they were helpless to act differently—not because of any limitations of their own but because of the limitations of others.

The manager listened carefully to the team members and tried to respond to their criticisms. He talked about the mistakes that he had made during the consulting process. For example, one professional objected to the way the manager had run the project meetings. "I see that the way I asked questions closed down discussions," responded the manager. "I didn't mean to do that, but I can see how you might have believed that I had already made up my mind." Another team member complained that the manager had caved in to pressure from his superior to produce the project report far too quickly, considering the team's heavy work load. "I think that it was my responsibility to have said no," admitted the manager. "It was clear that we all had an immense amount of work."

Finally, after some three hours of discussion about his own behavior, the manager began to ask the team members if there were any errors *they* might have made. "After all," he said, "this client was not different from many others. How can we be more effective in the future?"

The professionals repeated that it was really the clients' and their own managers' fault. As one put it, "They have to be open to change and want to learn." The more the manager tried to get the team to examine its own responsibility for the outcome, the more the professionals bypassed his concerns. The best one team member could suggest was for the case team to "promise less"—implying that there was really no way for the group to improve its performance.

The case team members were reacting defensively to protect themselves, even though their manager was not acting in ways that an outsider would consider threatening. Even if there were some truth to their charges—the clients may well have been arrogant and closed, their own managers distant—the way they presented these claims was guaranteed to stop learning. With few exceptions, the professionals made attributions about the behavior of the clients and the managers but never publicly tested their claims. For instance, they said that the clients weren't motivated to learn but never really presented any evidence supporting that assertion. When their lack of concrete evidence was pointed out to them, they simply repeated their criticisms more vehemently.

If the professionals had felt so strongly about these issues, why had they never mentioned them during the project? According to the professionals, even this was the fault of others. "We didn't want to alienate the client," argued one. "We didn't want to be seen as whining," said another.

The professionals were using their criticisms of others to protect themselves from the potential embarrassment of having to admit that perhaps they too had contributed to the team's less-than-perfect performance. What's more, the fact that they kept repeating their defensive actions in the face of the manager's efforts to turn the group's attention to its own role shows that this defensiveness had become a reflexive routine. From the professionals' perspective, they weren't resisting; they were focusing on the "real" causes. Indeed, they were to be respected, if not congratulated, for working as well as they did under such difficult conditions.

The end result was an unproductive parallel conversation. Both the manager and the professionals were candid; they expressed their views forcefully. But they talked past each other, never finding a common language to describe what had happened with the client. The professionals kept insisting that the fault lay with others. The manager kept trying, unsuccessfully, to get the professionals to see how they contributed to the state of affairs they were criticizing. The dialogue of this parallel conversation looks like this:

Professionals: "The clients have to be open. They must want to change."

Manager: "It's our task to help them see that change is in their interest."

Professionals: "But the clients didn't agree with our analyses."

Manager: "If they didn't think our ideas were right, how might we have convinced them?"

Professionals: "Maybe we need to have more meetings with the client."

Manager: "If we aren't adequately prepared and if the clients don't think we're credible, how will more meetings help?"

Professionals: "There should be better communication between case team members and management."

Manager: "I agree. But professionals should take the initiative to educate the manager about the problems they are experiencing."

Professionals: "Our leaders are unavailable and distant."

Manager: "How do you expect us to know that if you don't tell us?"

Conversations such as this one dramatically illustrate the learning dilemma. The problem with the professionals' claims is not that they are wrong but that they aren't useful. By constantly turning the focus away from their own behavior to that of others, the professionals bring learning to a grinding halt. The manager understands the trap but does not know how to get out of it. To learn how to do that requires going deeper into the dynamics of defensive reasoning—and into the special causes that make professionals so prone to it.

Defensive Reasoning and the Doom Loop

What explains the professionals' defensiveness? Not their attitudes about change or commitment to continuous improvement; they really wanted to work more effectively. Rather, the key factor is the way they reasoned about their behavior and that of others.

It is impossible to reason anew in every situation. If we had to think through all the possible responses every time someone asked, "How are you?" the world would pass us by. Therefore, everyone develops a theory of action—a set of rules that individuals use to design and implement their own behavior as well as to understand the behavior of others. Usually, these theories of actions become so taken for granted that people don't even realize they are using them.

One of the paradoxes of human behavior, however, is that the master program people actually use is rarely the one they think they use. Ask people in an interview or questionnaire to articulate the rules they use to govern their actions, and they will give you what I call their "espoused" theory of action. But observe these same people's behavior, and you will quickly see that this espoused theory has very little to do with how they actually behave. For example, the professionals on the case team said they believed in continuous improvement, and yet they consistently acted in ways that made improvement impossible.

When you observe people's behavior and try to come up with rules that would make sense of it, you discover a very different theory of action—what I call the individual's "theory-in-use." Put simply, people consistently act inconsistently, unaware of the contradiction between their espoused theory and their theory-in-use, between the way they think they are acting and the way they really act.

What's more, most theories-in-use rest on the same set of governing values. There seems to be a universal human tendency to design one's actions consistently according to four basic values:

1. To remain in unilateral control;

2. To maximize "winning" and minimize "losing";

3. To suppress negative feelings; and

4. To be as "rational" as possible—by which people mean defining clear objectives and evaluating their behavior in terms of whether or not they have achieved them.

The purpose of all these values is to avoid embarrassment or threat, feeling vulnerable or incompetent. In this respect, the master program that most people use is profoundly defensive. Defensive reasoning encourages individuals to keep private the premises, inferences, and conclusions that shape their behavior and to avoid testing them in a truly independent, objective fashion.

Because the attributions that go into defensive reasoning are never really tested, it is a closed loop, remarkably impervious to conflicting points of view. The inevitable response to the observation that somebody is reasoning defensively is yet more defensive reasoning. With the case team, for example, whenever anyone pointed out the professionals' defensive behavior to them, their initial reaction was to look for the cause in somebody else—clients who were so sensitive that they would have been alienated if the consultants had criticized them or a manager so weak that he couldn't have taken it had the consultants raised their concerns with him. In other words, the case team members once again denied their own responsibility by externalizing the problem and putting it on someone else.

In such situations, the simple act of encouraging more open inquiry is often attacked by others as "intimidating." Those who do the attacking deal with their feelings about possibly being wrong by blaming the more open individual for arousing these feelings and upsetting them.

Needless to say, such a master program inevitably short-circuits learning. And for a number of reasons unique to their psychology, well-educated professionals are especially susceptible to this.

Nearly all the consultants I have studied have stellar academic records. Ironically, their very success at education helps explain the problems they have with learning. Before they enter the world of work, their lives are primarily full of successes, so they have rarely experienced the embarrassment and sense of threat that comes with failure. As a result, their defensive reasoning has rarely been activated. People who rarely experience failure, however, end up not knowing how to deal with it effectively. And this serves to reinforce the normal human tendency to reason defensively.

In a survey of several hundred young consultants at the organizations I have been studying, these professionals describe themselves as driven internally by an unrealistically high ideal of performance: "Pressure on the job is self-imposed." "I must not only do a good job; I must also be the best." "People around here are very bright and hardworking; they are highly motivated to do an outstanding job." "Most of us want not only to succeed but also to do so at maximum speed."

These consultants are always comparing themselves with the best around them and constantly trying to better their own performance. And yet they do not appreciate being required to compete openly with each other. They feel it is somehow inhumane. They prefer to be the individual contributor—what might be termed a "productive loner."

Behind this high aspiration for success is an equally high fear of failure and a propensity to feel shame and guilt when they do fail to meet their high standards. "You must avoid mistakes," said one. "I hate making them. Many of us fear failure, whether we admit it or not."

To the extent that these consultants have experienced success in their lives, they have not had to be concerned about failure and the attendant feelings of shame and guilt. But to exactly the same extent, they also have never developed the tolerance for feelings of failure or the skills to deal with these feelings. This in turn has led them not only to fear failure but also to fear the fear of failure itself. For they know that they will not cope with it superlatively—their usual level of aspiration.

The consultants use two intriguing metaphors to describe this phenomenon. They talk about the "doom loop" and "doom zoom." Often, consultants will perform well on the case team, but because they don't do the jobs perfectly or receive accolades from their managers, they go into a doom loop of despair. And they don't ease into the doom loop, they zoom into it.

As a result, many professionals have extremely "brittle" personalities. When suddenly faced with a situation they cannot immediately handle, they tend to fall apart. They cover up their distress in front of the client. They talk about it constantly with their fellow case team members. Interestingly, these conversations commonly take the form of bad-mouthing clients.

Such brittleness leads to an inappropriately high sense of despondency or even despair when people don't achieve the high levels of performance they aspire to. Such despondency is rarely psychologically devastating, but when combined with defensive reasoning, it can result in a formidable predisposition against learning.

There is no better example of how this brittleness can disrupt an organization than performance evaluations. Because it represents the one moment when a professional must measure his or her own behavior against some formal standard, a performance evaluation is almost tailor-made to push a professional into the doom loop. Indeed, a poor evaluation can reverberate far beyond the particular individual involved to spark defensive reasoning throughout an entire organization.

At one consulting company, management established a new performance-evaluation process that was designed to make evaluations both more objective and more useful to those being evaluated. The consultants participated in the design of the new system and in general were enthusiastic because it corresponded to their espoused values of objectivity and fairness. A brief two years into the new process, however, it had become the object of dissatisfaction. The catalyst for this about-face was the first unsatisfactory rating.

Senior managers had identified six consultants whose performance they considered below standard. In keeping with the new evaluation process, they did all they could to communicate their concerns to the six and to help them improve. Managers met with each individual separately for as long and as often as the professional requested to explain the reasons behind the rating and to discuss what needed to be done to improve—but to no avail. Performance continued at the same low level and, eventually, the six were let go.

When word of the dismissal spread through the company, people responded with confusion and anxiety. After about a dozen consultants angrily complained to management, the CEO held two lengthy meetings where employees could air their concerns.

At the meetings, the professionals made a variety of claims. Some said the performance-evaluation process was unfair because judgments were subjective and biased and the criteria for minimum performance unclear. Others suspected that the real cause for the dismissals was economic and that the performance-evaluation procedure was just a fig leaf to hide the fact that the company was in trouble. Still others argued that the evaluation process was antilearning. If the company were truly a learning organization, as it claimed, then people performing below the minimum standard should be taught how to reach it. As one professional put it: "We were told that the company did not have an up-or-out policy. Up-or-out is inconsistent with learning. You misled us."

The CEO tried to explain the logic behind management's decision by grounding it in the facts of the case and by asking the professionals for any evidence that might contradict these facts.

Is there subjectivity and bias in the evaluation process? Yes, responded the CEO, but "we strive hard to reduce them. We are constantly trying to improve the process. If you have any ideas, please tell us. If you know of someone treated unfairly, please bring it up. If any of you feel that you have been treated unfairly, let's discuss it now or, if you wish, privately."

Is the level of minimum competence too vague? "We are working to define minimum competence more clearly," he answered. "In the case of the six, however, their performance was so poor that it wasn't difficult to reach a decision." Most of the six had received timely feedback about their problems. And in the two cases where people had not, the reason was that they had never taken the responsibility to seek out evaluations— and, indeed, had actively avoided them. "If you have any data to the contrary," the CEO added, "let's talk about it."

Were the six asked to leave for economic reasons? No, said the CEO. "We have more work than we can do, and letting professionals go is extremely costly for us. Do any of you have any information to the contrary?"

As to the company being antilearning, in fact, the entire evaluation process was designed to encourage learning. When a professional is performing below the minimum level, the CEO explained, "we jointly design remedial experiences with the individual. Then we look for signs of improvement. In these cases, either the professionals were reluctant to take on such assignments or they repeatedly failed when they did. Again, if you have information or evidence to the contrary, I'd like to hear about it."

The CEO concluded: "It's regrettable, but sometimes we make mistakes and hire the wrong people. If individuals don't produce and repeatedly prove themselves unable to improve, we don't know what else to do except dismiss them. It's just not fair to keep poorly performing individuals in the company. They earn an unfair share of the financial rewards."

Instead of responding with data of their own, the professionals simply repeated their accusations but in ways that consistently contradicted their claims. They said that a genuinely fair evaluation process would contain clear and documentable data about performance—but they were unable to provide firsthand examples of the unfairness that they implied colored the evaluation of the six dismissed employees. They argued that people shouldn't be judged by inferences unconnected to their actual performance—but they judged management in precisely this way. They insisted that management define clear, objective, and unambiguous performance standards—but they argued that any humane system would take into account that the performance of a professional cannot be precisely measured. Finally, they presented themselves as champions of learning—but they never proposed any criteria for assessing whether an individual might be unable to learn.

In short, the professionals seemed to hold management to a different level of performance than they held themselves. In their conversation at the meetings, they used many of the features of ineffective evaluation that they condemned—the absence of concrete data, for example, and the dependence on a circular logic of "heads we win, tails you lose." It is as if they were saying, "Here are the features of a fair performance-evaluation system. You should abide by them. But we don't have to when we are evaluating you."

Indeed, if we were to explain the professionals' behavior by articulating rules that would have to be in their heads in order for them to act the way they did, the rules would look something like this:

1. When criticizing the company, state your criticism in ways that you believe are valid—but also in ways that prevent others from deciding for themselves whether your claim to validity is correct.

2. When asked to illustrate your criticisms, don't include any data that others could use to decide for themselves whether the illustrations are valid.

3. State your conclusions in ways that disguise their logical implications. If others point out those implications to you, deny them.

Of course, when such rules were described to the professionals, they found them abhorrent. It was inconceivable that these rules might explain their actions. And yet in defending themselves against this observation, they almost always inadvertently confirmed the rules.

Learning How to Reason Productively

If defensive reasoning is as widespread as I believe, then focusing on an individual's attitudes or commitment is never enough to produce real change. And as the previous example illustrates, neither is creating new organizational structures or systems. The problem is that even when people are genuinely committed to improving their performance and management has changed its structures in order to encourage the "right" kind of behavior, people still remain locked in defensive reasoning. Either they remain unaware of this fact, or if they do become aware of it, they blame others.

There is, however, reason to believe that organizations can break out of this vicious circle. Despite the strength of defensive reasoning, people genuinely strive to produce what they intend. They value acting competently. Their self-esteem is intimately tied up with behaving consistently and performing effectively. Companies can use these universal human tendencies to teach people how to reason in a new way—in effect, to change the master programs in their heads and thus reshape their behavior.

People can be taught how to recognize the reasoning they use when they design and implement their actions.

They can begin to identify the inconsistencies between their espoused and actual theories of action. They can face up to the fact that they unconsciously design and implement actions that they do not intend. Finally, people can learn how to identify what individuals and groups do to create organizational defenses and how these defenses contribute to an organization's problems.

Once companies embark on this learning process, they will discover that the kind of reasoning necessary to reduce and overcome organizational defenses is the same kind of "tough reasoning" that underlies the effective use of ideas in strategy, finance, marketing, manufacturing, and other management disciplines. Any sophisticated strategic analysis, for example, depends on collecting valid data, analyzing it carefully, and constantly testing the inferences drawn from the data. The toughest tests are reserved for the conclusions. Good strategists make sure that their conclusions can withstand all kinds of critical questioning.

So too with productive reasoning about human behavior. The standard of analysis is just as high. Human resource programs no longer need to be based on "soft" reasoning but should be as analytical and as data-driven as any other management discipline.

Of course, that is not the kind of reasoning the consultants used when they encountered problems that were embarrassing or threatening. The data they collected was hardly objective. The inferences they made rarely became explicit. The conclusions they reached were largely self-serving, impossible for others to test, and as a result, "self-sealing," impervious to change.

How can an organization begin to turn this situation around, to teach its members how to reason productively? The first step is for managers at the top to examine critically and change their own theories-in-use. Until senior managers become aware of how they reason defensively and the counterproductive consequences that result, there will be little real progress. Any change activity is likely to be just a fad.

Change has to start at the top because otherwise defensive senior managers are likely to disown any transformation in reasoning patterns coming from below. If professionals or middle managers begin to change the way they reason and act, such changes are likely to appear strange—if not actually dangerous—to those at the top. The result is an unstable situation where senior managers still believe that it is a sign of caring and sensitivity to bypass and cover up difficult issues, while their subordinates see the very same actions as defensive.

The key to any educational experience designed to teach senior managers how to reason productively is to connect the program to real business problems. The best demonstration of the usefulness of productive reasoning is for busy managers to see how it can make a direct difference in their own performance and in that of the organization. This will not happen overnight. Managers need plenty of opportunity to practice the new skills. But once they grasp the powerful impact that productive reasoning can have on actual performance, they will have a strong incentive to reason productively not just in a training session but in all their work relationships.

One simple approach I have used to get this process started is to have participants produce a kind of rudimentary case study. The subject is a real business problem that the manager either wants to deal with or has tried unsuccessfully to address in the past. Writing the actual case usually takes less than an hour. But then the case becomes the focal point of an extended analysis.

For example, a CEO at a large organizational-development consulting company was preoccupied with the problems caused by the intense competition among the various business functions represented by his four direct reports. Not only was he tired of having the problems dumped in his lap, but he was also worried about the impact the interfunctional conflicts were having on the organization's flexibility. He had even calculated that the money being spent to iron out disagreements amounted to hundreds of thousands of dollars every year. And the more fights there were, the more defensive people became, which only increased the costs to the organization.

In a paragraph or so, the CEO described a meeting he intended to have with his direct reports to address the problem. Next, he divided the paper in half, and on the right-hand side of the page, he wrote a scenario for the meeting—much like the script for a movie or play—describing what he would say and how his subordinates would likely respond. On the left-hand side of the page, he wrote down any thoughts and feelings that he would be likely to have during the meeting but that he wouldn't express for fear they would derail the discussion.

But instead of holding the meeting, the CEO analyzed this scenario *with* his direct reports. The case became the catalyst for a discussion in which the CEO learned several things about the way he acted with his management team.

He discovered that his four direct reports often perceived his conversations as counterproductive. In the guise of being "diplomatic," he would pretend that a consensus about the problem existed, when in fact none existed. The unintended result: instead of feeling reassured, his subordinates felt wary and tried to figure out "what is he *really* getting at."

The CEO also realized that the way he dealt with the competitiveness among department heads was completely contradictory. On the one hand, he kept urging them to "think of the organization as a whole." On the other, he kept calling for actions—department budget cuts, for example—that placed them directly in competition with each other.

Finally, the CEO discovered that many of the tacit evaluations and attributions he had listed turned out to be wrong. Since he had never expressed these assumptions, he had never found out just how wrong they were. What's more, he learned that much of what he thought he was hiding came through to his subordinates anyway—but with the added message that the boss was covering up.

The CEO's colleagues also learned about their own ineffective behavior. They learned by examining their own behavior as they tried to help the CEO analyze his case. They also learned by writing and analyzing cases of their own. They began to see that they too tended to bypass and cover up the real issues and that the CEO was often aware of it but did not say so. They too made inaccurate attributions and evaluations that they did not express. Moreover, the belief that they had to hide important ideas and feelings from the CEO and from each other in order not to upset anyone turned out to be mistaken. In the context of the case discussions, the entire senior management team was quite willing to discuss what had always been undiscussable.

In effect, the case study exercise legitimizes talking about issues that people have never been able to address before. Such a discussion can be emotional—even painful. But for managers with the courage to persist, the payoff is great: management teams and entire organizations work more openly and more effectively and have greater options for behaving flexibly and adapting to particular situations.

When senior managers are trained in new reasoning skills, they can have a big impact on the performance of the entire organization—even when other employees are still reasoning defensively. The CEO who led the meetings on the performance-evaluation procedure was able to defuse dissatisfaction because he didn't respond to professionals' criticisms in kind but instead gave a clear presentation of relevant data. Indeed, most participants took the CEO's behavior to be a sign that the company really acted on the values of participation and employee involvement that it espoused.

Of course, the ideal is for all the members of an organization to learn how to reason productively. This has happened at the company where the case team meeting took place. Consultants and their managers are now able to confront some of the most difficult issues of the consultant-client relationship. To get a sense of the difference productive reasoning can make, imagine how the original conversation between the manager and case team might have gone had everyone engaged in effective reasoning. (The following dialogue is based on actual sessions I have attended with other case teams at the same company since the training has been completed.)

First, the consultants would have demonstrated their commitment to continuous improvement by being willing to examine their own role in the difficulties that arose during the consulting project. No doubt they would have identified their managers and the clients as part of the problem, but they would have gone on to admit that they had contributed to it as well. More important, they would have agreed with the manager that as they explored the various roles of clients, managers, and professionals, they would make sure to test any evaluations or attributions they might make against the data. Each individual would have encouraged the others to question his or her reasoning. Indeed, they would have insisted on it. And in turn, everyone would have understood that act of questioning not as a sign of mistrust or an invasion of privacy but as a valuable opportunity for learning.

The conversation about the manager's unwillingness to say no might look something like this:

Professional #1: "One of the biggest problems I had with the way you managed this case was that you seemed to be unable to say no when either the client or your superior made unfair demands." [Gives an example.]

Professional #2: "I have another example to add. [Describes a second example.] But I'd also like to say that we never really told you how we felt about this. Behind your back we were bad-mouthing you—you know, 'he's being such a wimp'—but we never came right out and said it."

Manager: "It certainly would have been helpful if you had said something. Was there anything I said or did that gave you the idea that you had better not raise this with me?"

Professional #3: "Not really. I think we didn't want to sound like we were whining."

Manager: "Well, I certainly don't think you sound like you're whining. But two thoughts come to mind. If I understand you correctly, you *were* complaining, but the complaining about me and my inability to say no was covered up. Second, if we had discussed this, I might have gotten the data I needed to be able to say no."

Notice that when the second professional describes how the consultants had covered up their complaints, the manager doesn't criticize her. Rather, he rewards her for being open by responding in kind. He focuses on the ways that he too may have contributed to the cover-up. Reflecting undefensively about his own role in the problem then makes it possible for the professionals to talk about their fears of appearing to be whining. The manager then agrees with the professionals that they shouldn't become complainers. At the same time, he points out the counterproductive consequences of covering up their complaints.

Another unresolved issue in the case team meeting concerned the supposed arrogance of the clients. A more productive conversation about that problem might go like this:

Manager: "You said that the clients were arrogant and uncooperative. What did they say and do?"

Professional #1: "One asked me if I had ever met a payroll. Another asked how long I've been out of school."

Professional #2: "One even asked me how old I was!"

Professional #3: "That's nothing. The worst is when they say that all we do is interview people, write a report based on what they tell us, and then collect our fees."

Manager: "The fact that we tend to be so young is a real problem for many of our clients. They get very defensive about it. But I'd like to explore whether there is a way for them to freely express their views without our getting defensive . . ."

"What troubled me about your original responses was that you assumed you were right in calling the clients stupid. One thing I've noticed about consultants—in this company and others—is that we tend to defend ourselves by bad-mouthing the client."

Professional #1: "Right. After all, if they are genuinely stupid, then it's obviously not our fault that they aren't getting it!"

Professional #2 "Of course, that stance is antilearning and overprotective. By assuming that they can't learn, we absolve ourselves from having to."

Professional #3: "And the more we all go along with the bad-mouthing, the more we reinforce each other's defensiveness."

Manager: "So what's the alternative? How can we encourage our clients to express their defensiveness and at the same time constructively build on it?"

Professional #1: "We all know that the real issue isn't our age; it's whether or not we are able to add value to the client's organization. They should judge us by what we produce. And if we aren't adding value, they should get rid of us—no matter how young or old we happen to be."

Manager: "Perhaps that is exactly what we should tell them."

In both these examples, the consultants and their manager are doing real work. They are learning about their own group dynamics and addressing some generic problems in client-consultant relationships. The insights they gain will allow them to act more effectively in the future—both as individuals and as a team. They are not just solving problems but developing a far deeper and more textured understanding of their role as members of the organization. They are laying the groundwork for continuous improvement that is truly continuous. They are learning how to learn.

Originally published in May 1991
Reprint 91301

Why Entrepreneurs Don't Scale

JOHN HAMM

Executive Summary

IT'S WELL KNOWN THAT MANY executives who excel
at starting businesses or projects fizzle out—in other
words, they fail to "scale"—as their ventures grow. But the
reasons have remained fuzzy.

In this article, leadership coach John Hamm identi-
fies four management tendencies that work for small-
company or business-unit leaders but become Achilles'
heels as those individuals try to run larger organizations. The first tendency is loyalty to comrades. In
entrepreneurial mode, you need to lead as though
you're in charge of a combat unit on the wrong side
of enemy lines. But blind loyalty can become a liability
in managing a complex organization. The second tendency, task orientation, is critical in driving toward a
big product launch, but excessive attention to detail
can cause a large organization to lose sight of its

long-term goals. The third tendency, single-mindedness, is important in a visionary unleashing a revolutionary product or service on the world but can limit the company's potential as it grows. And the fourth tendency, working in isolation, is fine for the brilliant scientist focused on an ingenious idea. But it's disastrous for a leader whose expanding organization increasingly relies on many other people.

Leaders who scale deal honestly with problems and quickly weed out nonperformers. They see past distractions and establish strategic priorities. They learn how to deal effectively with diverse employees, customers, and external constituencies. And, most important, they make the company's continuing health and welfare their top concern.

It's a cliché to say that founders flounder, but unfortunately, that's usually the case. Wild exceptions like Bill Gates, Steve Jobs, and Michael Dell aside, executives who start a business or project fizzle more often than not once they've gotten their venture on its feet.

Entrepreneurs actually show their inability to switch to executive mode much earlier in the business development process than most people realize, as my stories will reveal. But the reasons executives fail to "scale"—that is, adapt their leadership capabilities to their growing businesses' needs—remain fuzzy. It's simply assumed that there's an entrepreneurial personality and an executive personality—and never the twain shall meet. I don't think that's true. I believe most executives can learn to scale if they're willing to take a step back and admit to themselves that their old ways no longer work.

Over the past four years, I've worked closely with more than 100 entrepreneurs and seen them struggle to adapt as their companies grow beyond a handful of employees and launch a new product or service. In the process, I've observed that the habits and skills that make entrepreneurs successful can undermine their ability to lead larger organizations. The problem, in other words, is not so much one of leadership personality as of approach. A leader who scales is able to jettison habits and skills that have outlived their usefulness and adapt to new challenges along the way.

I've identified four tendencies that work for leaders of business units or small companies but become Achilles' heels for those same individuals when they try to manage larger organizations with diverse needs, departments, priorities, and constituencies.

The first tendency is loyalty to comrades—the small band of colleagues there at the start of the enterprise. In entrepreneurial mode, you need to lead like you're in charge of a combat unit on the wrong side of enemy lines, where it's all for one and one for all. But blind loyalty can become a liability in managing a large, complex organization. The second tendency, task orientation—or focusing on the job at hand—is critical in driving toward, say, a big product launch, but excessive attention to detail can cause a large organization to lose its way. The third tendency, single-mindedness, is an important attribute in a visionary who wants to unleash a revolutionary product or service on the world. Yet this quality can harden into tunnel vision if the leader can't become more expansive as the company grows. And the fourth tendency, working in isolation, is fine for the brilliant scientist focused on an ingenious idea. But it's disastrous for a leader whose burgeoning organization must rely on the kindness of customers, investors, analysts, reporters, and other strangers.

Leaders who scale overcome these tendencies by dint of self-discipline, listening to and seeking input from others, and being willing to shift their outlook. They deal honestly with problems and quickly weed out nonperformers. They see past distractions and establish strategic priorities. They make concerted, sometimes uncomfortable efforts to do what doesn't come naturally to them for the team's sake. And they learn to work with and communicate to diverse employees, customers, and external constituencies. Most important, they make the company's continuing health and welfare their top concern.

The following stories are about CEOs of technology start-ups, and they're composites of individuals with whom I've worked as an investor, board member, and coach. (The CEOs have all been given pseudonyms here.) Technology start-ups make good case studies because their lack of bureaucracy, compressed product development time, intense relationships, and vulnerability to bottom-line vicissitudes throw leadership challenges into high relief. They yield lessons that apply not only to entrepreneurs as their companies grow but also to project or department leaders as they take on bigger responsibilities in organizations of any size. As we shall see, the ability to effectively lead a project, department, or organization beyond the start-up stage depends on whether or not the executive is hampered by the four hazardous tendencies outlined here.

The Scaling Challenge

Business school courses can't really teach students to deal with people objectively, to think strategically, to create loyalty within a diverse workforce, and to impress customers and investors. These capabilities derive from experience that the new CEO may not yet have. No wonder so many entrepreneurs fail to become self-sufficient leaders as their businesses increase in complexity.

Without these skills, most new CEOs fall back on what has worked well for them before—even though these old approaches often don't fit the current problem. A product manager turned CEO may believe the next product will turn a profit. An entrepreneur who cut his teeth in marketing may respond to increasing competition with a new ad campaign. Faced with shrinking revenues, an accountant who's started a company may focus on reducing costs.

But most often, the fledgling CEOs I've observed fall into some of the traps outlined below, any one of which can be fatal to a leader's career, and even to the company being led. These entrepreneurs aren't aware that by clinging to their existing strengths and habits, they risk creating dysfunctional companies. See "Testing for Scalability" for more information.

Let's examine the four tendencies that can prevent executives from scaling.

LOYALTY TO COMRADES

Excessively loyal CEOs may be the best friends you could ever have, but they are the growing organization's worst enemies. That fault is understandable enough; after all, team allegiance significantly contributes to company success. But when leaders fail to see and respond to a team member's weaknesses, they place the company at risk.

Take Jason, the founder of a company specializing in wireless technology. Jason was enthusiastic and tireless

Testing for Scalability

If you're thinking about turning an entrepreneur into a large-company CEO, look before you leap. A prospect can seem stunning on paper or during an interview but can disappoint in practice. The following questions can help reveal what's beneath the surface.

Question:	To Determine:	To Test for:
1. Have you ever fired someone? Describe what happened.	How quickly does the candidate deal with nonperformers?	loyalty
2. Pick three priorities from a sample list of ten.	Does the candidate think strategically?	task orientation
3. Describe a situation in which you were wrong and how you dealt with it.	Does the candidate learn from humbling experiences?	single-mindedness
4. What do you see as your external role in this position?	Is the candidate interested in evangelizing?	working in isolation
5. Describe your dream house.	Does the candidate have visionary capacity?	task orientation
6. What was the scariest moment in your professional career?	Is the candidate courageous?	single-mindedness
7. If you had to fire either your marketing or engineering VP, whom would you fire first?	Does the candidate protect like-minded people?	loyalty
8. What would you do if your top salesperson was distracted, and sales were falling apart as a result?	Can the candidate separate performance issues from excuses?	loyalty
9. What did you like and dislike about your last job?	Does the candidate blame others? Is he or she enriched by experience?	single-mindedness, loyalty
10. If you could return to school and study something new, what would it be?	Is the candidate a curious learner?	single-mindedness

in recruiting his start-up team of 20. As a loyal comrade to the cadre of smart engineers he'd befriended in graduate school and kept in touch with over the years, Jason was able to tap into his old-buddy network to build a highly competent team. Among Jason's friends was Mark, an engineering professional with whom he had never worked but felt confident would be a brilliant hire. That's because Mark had previously been a technical development manager for a large enterprise-software company. Jason courted Mark assiduously, enticing him with the opportunity to influence the start-up's strategy and make a pile of money if the venture was successful. When Mark decided to take the job, Jason was thrilled.

At first, Mark seemed like an excellent fit. He was enthusiastic about the technology, and people loved working for him. But as the company prepared to launch its first product, Mark's team wasn't equal to the engineering challenge. Accustomed to more development time and a larger staff, Mark was unable to keep up with his job's demands, and his team failed to meet a critical product milestone.

When a board member first raised the subject of Mark's performance, Jason responded with airy promises: "We're almost there with the code freeze," and "We just need another round of tests." When pressed, Jason made excuses. He insisted that Mark was working very hard, the technology was complex, and the competition was stiff. Jason refused to fire his friend even after competitors beat the company to market with a wireless product that quickly became the industry's de facto standard. Revenues took a nosedive. Then came the layoffs. Eventually, the investors shut down the company.

Such stubborn loyalty, at the expense of an organization's success, is surprisingly common. But leaders who scale, while not lacking in sympathy toward individuals, understand that the organization's success depends on every team member's strengths. These leaders understand that their first allegiance must be to a broad community of employees, customers, and investors, and to the fundamentals of the business—not to any single friend.

A good example of a leader who didn't let loyalty stand in the way of smart business is Sandy, the CEO of a small but growing organization that provides DSL broadband service. Like Jason, Sandy was a loyal friend to people she'd known since her career began. She brought in an affable, outgoing college chum, Mike, to run the startup's technical sales department. After six months on the job, however, Sandy began to suspect that Mike needed to be more aggressive. Though he had responded to some requests for proposals, he often didn't follow up. When a promising prospect passed over Sandy's company in favor of a competitor that had an inferior product, Sandy started asking questions. First, she approached Anne, one of Mike's sales managers, about his performance. Visibly upset, Anne complained that she'd had to pick up Mike's slack; 80-hour weeks had taken their toll, and she wasn't sure how much longer she could keep up the pace. Next, Sandy checked with the CFO, who didn't deliver any better news about Mike's performance. If Mike wasn't able to clinch a deal with a very important prospect, the CFO said, the company would miss a huge revenue opportunity necessary to meet expenses.

Sandy decided that Mike had to go, but she wasn't cold about it. Empathetic and respectful, Sandy made it clear that their partnership just wasn't working. She acknowledged that Mike had left a great job to join her start-up, but now it was flirting with failure. After laying out the details of the potentially disastrous situation, she said she had no choice but to terminate Mike's employment, explaining that her decision was nothing personal and she hoped they would remain friends. When Mike left, Sandy became acting head of technical sales until she found a replacement. The company survived.

TASK ORIENTATION

Executives who focus on the job at hand—particularly those who have done well in operations, product development, or finance—are the weight lifters of the business world. They execute brilliantly with demanding short-term assignments, but long-term strategy is often beyond them. As their companies grow, they often fail to establish strategic priorities.

Marvin, an enormously ambitious CEO of a Web services company, was that type of executive. Armed with an advanced degree in computer science, he ran product development for a firm that held a successful IPO during the dot-com era. After cashing in his stock options, Marvin pursued his dream of founding his own company.

At the outset, Marvin's task-oriented style served him well. He hired an impressive core team of engineers and set them to work on one critical task: developing a working prototype for a clearly differentiated product. Marvin's intense focus on this effort impressed venture capitalists, who rewarded him with a generous first round of financing.

As the company put out the product and expanded to 95 people, Marvin's to-do list grew. His long list of "critical" items included cutting a deal with Dell, hiring a sales VP, getting a big-name CEO on the board of directors, setting a strategy for further technology development, moving into new offices, and launching an intensive public relations and advertising campaign. Marvin delegated all these tasks to department managers, then rode herd on them. Twice a week, he required managers to update him on their projects' status. Employees made progress, but Marvin abhorred a vacuum: As soon as they completed one task, he'd fill their lists again. At first, the staff enjoyed being so busy. But within six months, people began to feel overwhelmed. Adding to their frustration was the fact that all final decisions had to pass through Marvin, who refused to make trade-offs. To him, all tasks demanded equal focus. Processes slowed. The marketing plan drifted.

No one was more dismayed or surprised than Marvin when a competitor beat his company to market with a new product and inked a significant deal with Dell. And no one was more to blame. In confusing tasks with goals, Marvin had lost control of his company's direction. The organization muddled along as a third-tier player until a competitor acquired the company at a bargain-basement price.

Leaders able to scale, by contrast, understand the importance of a streamlined strategy. They learn to extract three or four high-level goals from a longer list and focus their teams accordingly. And in the face of a new threat or opportunity, they release people from promises that were made at a different point in the development process, allowing them to delay or cancel goals they had committed to when they made sense.

Harry, the founder of a small content-management company, understood that a well-developed, simple strategy is the most important pillar of any business. He knew that his company first needed to focus on beating the competition and thus urged employees to concentrate on three activities in service to that goal: consolidating product lines, winning business away from a particularly fierce rival, and focusing on selling to companies with at least 1,000 users. This was Harry's mantra, and he repeated it at every opportunity, every day, to everyone.

That's not to say Harry's company left all other important tasks undone. Rather, Harry let employees set them aside so they could concentrate on the primary goal of beating the competition. For example, when it became clear the sales department had been focusing on customers of various sizes—many small, a few medium, and three large—Harry told the salespeople to forget about small customers.

Now, Harry understood that his strategy might be off the mark. After all, he had no crystal ball telling him that the direction he had chosen was the right one. So he availed himself of that rudder on which scalable leaders rely: the quarterly strategy audit. Every three months, Harry gathered the company's senior managers, directors, advisers, and business colleagues to review current strategy. During the four-hour meeting, the group would force itself to distill, from a list of ten, three key initiatives to be accomplished during the next 90 days. The most difficult part of the process was letting go of the remaining seven initiatives on the list. Still, the group emerged having established a simple, yet well-thought-out, plan that every employee could easily understand and follow and that could be altered the subsequent quarter, if need be. As one executive stated, "We might be wrong, but we aren't confused."

Harry was able to scale because he learned to focus on what was crucial and, in doing so, he could balance competing forces in order to set clear goals for his employees. In many ways, Harry mirrored the approaches of scalable founders-cum-leaders like Dell and Gates, who have been willing to halt extraneous activities and refocus all efforts on a few key accomplishments.

SINGLE-MINDEDNESS

We all admire disciplined people, and in start-ups, laser-like focus on the quality and differentiation of a new product or service is an important asset. But a leader's devotion to a single issue can also damage a growing organization. An insulated leader who doesn't communicate with and listen to employees with distinct opinions can end up losing their allegiance.

Sanjit, the founder of a company specializing in fiber-optic systems, was a serious technologist deeply involved with the theoretical aspects of his organization's industry niche. During the start-up stage, Sanjit's obsession was invaluable: Investors were very impressed with his understanding of and belief in the technology. His passion also appealed to the group of ten like-minded technologists he'd hired to build the company's breakthrough products. Because they shared his vision, Sanjit didn't have to spend a lot of time rallying the troops or discussing the company's strategy. His team members were convinced that when their product entered the market, it would be a runaway hit. Their enthusiasm and energy were palpable.

But as the company recruited a more diverse workforce to handle sales and run operations, Sanjit remained absorbed in the technology alone. Indeed, he had no interest in anything aside from fiber optics. He dismissed, ignored, or openly criticized marketers, salespeople, and administrators who failed to appreciate the finer points of the company's technology. And he ended up with unhappy employees, many of whom arrived not a minute before nine and left at the stroke of five each day. They gossiped about one another and picked interdepartmental quarrels. Marketers blamed technical writers for not providing data-sheet information; tech writers blamed engineers for failing to provide specifications; engineers blamed product managers for dragging their feet with outside partners. Meanwhile, the company failed to attract intelligent contributors or keep the ones it had. Like Marvin's Web services company, Sanjit's organization limped along until it was acquired for next to nothing.

Sanjit sacrificed employee loyalty to his own single-mindedness. By contrast, executives who scale learn to listen to others and take their opinions into account. They grow with their companies because they realize that their passion is not the only one that matters, and they intentionally broaden their perspective to encompass a range of endeavors.

Todd was a CEO who could see beyond his own area of interest. He was an engineer whose start-up developed and marketed software applications for wireless devices. Like Sanjit, Todd was fascinated by the technology and fervently believed that his software concept was not only groundbreaking but also potentially world changing. In response to such enthusiasm, investors wrote him substantial checks.

As the company grew, however, Todd realized that it could not live on technological excellence alone. So, unlike Sanjit, Todd paid more attention to issues that didn't revolve around the technology. He asked the public relations manager, for example, to explain how reporters thought and worked; he encouraged salespeople to describe their customer interactions. Each Friday,

Todd held an all-hands meeting outlining progress toward goals and publicly acknowledging the good work of contributors, including administrative assistants and shipping clerks. And in working with his direct reports, Todd stressed the importance of making team members feel valued.

By seeking input and information from others, Todd deepened his understanding of their agendas and concerns. Because he encouraged coworkers to take pride in their contributions, they rewarded him with renewed commitment. In the end, his company scored an impressive second round of financing and secured major deals that placed it at the top of its sector.

WORKING IN ISOLATION

An embryonic idea demands protection; in fact, the gestational development itself is excitingly secretive. But after the birth of the product or the idea, the internal focus must shift, lest it impede responsiveness to market demands for the finished product.

David, the founder of a software company focusing on e-mail security, was a talented programmer who enjoyed working with his engineering group on developing the first product. An introvert by nature, David liked to work in the cloistered start-up environment, where everyone was devoted to the product. David's diffidence didn't bother his few employees. Nor did he feel the need to impress anyone outside his company. Because the organization was small, and because David and his friends and family were the sole investors, he didn't need to reach out.

Then the time came to launch and market the product, and David found all kinds of ways to remain sequestered. As production deadlines loomed, he extended development cutoff dates. He tweaked packaging copy "just one more time." He canceled meetings with the public relations agency arranging press and analyst meetings. When a reporter called for a prearranged interview, David made sure he was in a meeting. Exasperated, his marketing director finally volunteered to deal with the press in David's place. As a result of David's refusal to meet with journalists, the new product was ranked as an also-ran in an important magazine review. Eventually, the board replaced David with someone more comfortable in the evangelist role.

Introverted entrepreneurs are often brilliant, but leaders who endure know that success requires some gladhanding and that they have to present their company to the world. Consider Simon, CEO of a small biotech company. A biochemist by training and an introvert by nature, Simon spent his professional career in large corporate research labs before being tapped to head a biotech spinout. His ability to hunker down with his team in the lab helped get the start-up's flagship product off the ground.

A year into his tenure, Simon realized that the sales reps were targeting the wrong people in customer organizations. They were selling to midlevel managers, not directors and vice presidents. Sales sagged and the company was running out of capital as a result. Simon realized that he'd better start meeting with new investors, customers, analysts, and the media before it was too late.

Simon forced himself to become a public face for the company. He worked with a media strategist to develop an action plan. He hired a coach who taught him how to appear confident and natural in press interviews. He cold-called both customers and large investment banks.

He also contacted top-level salespeople in public companies, persuading two of them to join his team. And when
a large customer had to choose between his and a competitor's offerings, Simon stepped in and helped close the
sale.

Flounder or Fly?

Clearly, addressing the problems of loyalty to comrades,
task orientation, single-mindedness, and working in isolation during a company's formative stages will allow the
founder to flourish over the long haul. On rare occasions,
people rise to the scaling challenge without any special
effort. More often, those who scale do so with outside
help—say, the feedback of an involved board member, a
coach, a mentor, or a facilitator. But entrepreneurs who
grow into leaders almost always scale because they are
open to learning. They want to be molded by new experiences and to improve their leadership selves. In fact,
leaders who scale do so regardless of background, skill,
and talent. Rather, they scale because they take deliber-
ate steps to confront their shortcomings and become the
leaders their organizations need them to be. Instead of
floundering, they learn to fly.

Originally published in December 2002
Reprint R0212J

The Making of a
Corporate Athlete

JIM LOEHR AND TONY SCHWARTZ

Executive Summary

MANAGEMENT THEORISTS HAVE long sought to identify precisely what makes some people flourish under
pressure and others fold. But they have come up with
only partial answers: rich material rewards, the right culture, management by objectives. The problem with most
approaches is that they deal with people only from the
neck up, connecting high performance primarily with
cognitive capacity. Authors Loehr and Schwartz argue
that a successful approach to sustained high performance must consider the person as a whole. Executives
are, in effect, "corporate athletes." If they are to perform
at high levels over the long haul, they must train in the
systematic, multilevel way that athletes do.

Rooted in two decades of work with world-class athletes, the integrated theory of performance management
addresses the body, the emotions, the mind, and the

127

spirit through a model the authors call the performance pyramid. At its foundation is physical well-being. Above that rest emotional health, then mental acuity, and, finally, a spiritual purpose. Each level profoundly influences the others, and all must be addressed together to avoid compromising performance. Rigorous exercise, for instance, can produce a sense of emotional well-being, clearing the way for peak mental performance. Rituals that promote oscillation—the rhythmic expenditure and recovery of energy—link the levels of the pyramid and lead to the ideal performance state.

The authors offer case studies of executives who have used the model to increase professional performance and improve the quality of their lives. In a corporate environment that is changing at warp speed, performing consistently at high levels is more necessary than ever. Companies can't afford to address employees' cognitive capacities while ignoring their physical, emotional, and spiritual well-being.

IF THERE IS ONE QUALITY THAT executives seek for themselves and their employees, it is sustained high performance in the face of ever-increasing pressure and rapid change. But the source of such performance is as elusive as the fountain of youth. Management theorists have long sought to identify precisely what makes some people flourish under pressure and others fold. We maintain that they have come up with only partial answers: rich material rewards, the right culture, management by objectives.

The problem with most approaches, we believe, is that they deal with people only from the neck up, connecting high performance primarily with cognitive capacity. In recent years there has been a growing focus on the relationship between emotional intelligence and high performance. A few theorists have addressed the spiritual dimension—how deeper values and a sense of purpose influence performance. Almost no one has paid any attention to the role played by physical capacities. A successful approach to sustained high performance, we have found, must pull together all of these elements and consider the person as a whole. Thus, our integrated theory of performance management addresses the body, the emotions, the mind, and the spirit. We call this hierarchy the *performance pyramid*. Each of its levels profoundly influences the others, and failure to address any one of them compromises performance.

Our approach has its roots in the two decades that Jim Loehr and his colleagues at LGE spent working with world-class athletes. Several years ago, the two of us began to develop a more comprehensive version of these techniques for executives facing unprecedented demands in the workplace. In effect, we realized, these executives are "corporate athletes." If they were to perform at high levels over the long haul, we posited, they would have to train in the same systematic, multilevel way that world-class athletes do. We have now tested our model on thousands of executives (see "The High-Performance Pyramid" for more detail). Their dramatically improved work performance and their enhanced health and happiness confirm our initial hypothesis. In the pages that follow, we describe our approach in detail.

Ideal Performance State

In training athletes, we have never focused on their primary skills—how to hit a serve, swing a golf club, or shoot a basketball. Likewise, in business we don't address primary competencies such as public speaking, negotiating, or analyzing a balance sheet. Our efforts aim instead to help executives build their capacity for what might be called supportive or secondary competencies, among them endurance, strength, flexibility, self-control, and focus. Increasing capacity at all levels allows athletes

The High-Performance Pyramid

Peak performance in business has often been presented as a matter of sheer brainpower, but we view performance as a pyramid. Physical well-being is its foundation. Above that rests emotional health, then mental acuity, and at the top, a sense of purpose. The Ideal Performance State—peak performance under pressure—is achieved when all levels are working together.

Rituals that promote oscillation—the rhythmic expenditure and recovery of energy—link the levels of the pyramid. For instance, vigorous exercise can produce a sense of emotional well-being, clearing the way for peak mental performance.

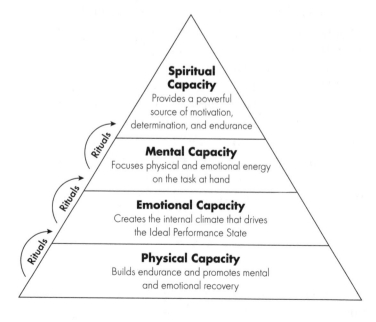

and executives alike to bring their talents and skills to full ignition and to sustain high performance over time—a condition we call the *Ideal Performance State* (IPS). Obviously, executives can perform successfully even if they smoke, drink and weigh too much, or lack emotional skills or a higher purpose for working. But they cannot perform to their full potential or without a cost over time—to themselves, to their families, and to the corporations for which they work. Put simply, the best long-term performers tap into positive energy at all levels of the performance pyramid.

Extensive research in sports science has confirmed that the capacity to mobilize energy on demand is the foundation of IPS. Our own work has demonstrated that effective energy management has two key components. The first is the rhythmic movement between energy expenditure (stress) and energy renewal (recovery), which we term "oscillation." In the living laboratory of sports, we learned that the real enemy of high performance is not stress, which, paradoxical as it may seem, is actually the stimulus for growth. Rather, the problem is the absence of disciplined, intermittent recovery. Chronic stress without recovery depletes energy reserves, leads to burnout and breakdown, and ultimately undermines performance. Rituals that promote oscillation—rhythmic stress and recovery—are the second component of high performance. Repeated regularly, these highly precise, consciously developed routines become automatic over time.

The same methods that enable world-class athletes to reach IPS under pressure, we theorized, would be at least equally effective for business leaders—and perhaps even more important in their lives. The demands on executives to sustain high performance day in and day out, year in and year out, dwarf the challenges faced by any athlete we have ever trained. The average professional athlete, for example, spends most of his time practicing and only a small percentage—several hours a day, at most—actually competing. The typical executive, by contrast, devotes almost no time to training and must perform on demand 10, 12, 14 hours a day or more. Athletes enjoy several months of off-season, while most executives are fortunate to get three or four weeks of vacation a year. The career of the average professional athlete spans seven years; the average executive can expect to work 40 to 50 years.

Of course, even corporate athletes who train at all levels will have bad days and run into challenges they can't overcome. Life is tough, and for many time-starved executives, it is only getting tougher. But that is precisely our point. While it isn't always in our power to change our external conditions, we can train to better manage our inner state. We aim to help corporate athletes use the full range of their capacities to thrive in the most difficult circumstances and to emerge from stressful periods stronger, healthier, and eager for the next challenge.

Physical Capacity

Energy can be defined most simply as the capacity to do work. Our training process begins at the physical level because the body is our fundamental source of energy—the foundation of the performance pyramid. Perhaps the best paradigm for building capacity is weight lifting. Several decades of sports science research have established that the key to increasing physical strength is a phenomenon known as supercompensation—essentially the creation of balanced work-rest ratios. In weight lifting, this involves stressing a muscle to the point where its fibers literally start to break down. Given an adequate period of recovery (typically at least 48 hours), the muscle will not only heal, it will grow stronger. But persist in stressing the muscle without rest and the result will be acute and chronic damage. Conversely, failure to stress the muscle results in weakness and atrophy. (Just think of an arm in a cast for several weeks.) In both cases, the enemy is not stress, it's linearity—the failure to oscillate between energy expenditure and recovery.

We first understood the power of rituals to prompt recovery by observing world-class tennis players in the crucible of match play. The best competitors, we discovered, use precise recovery rituals in the 15 or 20 seconds *between* points—often without even being aware of it. Their between-point routines include concentrating on the strings of their rackets to avoid distraction, assuming a confident posture, and visualizing how they want the next point to play out. These routines have startling physiological effects. When we hooked players up to heart rate monitors during their matches, the competitors with the most consistent rituals showed dramatic oscillation, their heart rates rising rapidly during play and then dropping as much as 15% to 20% between points.

The mental and emotional effects of precise between-point routines are equally significant. They allow players to avoid negative feelings, focus their minds, and prepare for the next point. By contrast, players who lack between-point rituals, or who practice them inconsistently, become linear—they expend too much energy without recovery. Regardless of their talent or level of fitness, they become more vulnerable to frustration, anxiety, and loss of concentration and far more likely to choke under pressure.

The same lesson applies to the corporate athletes we train. The problem, we explain, is not so much that their lives are increasingly stressful as that they are so relentlessly linear. Typically, they push themselves too hard mentally and emotionally and too little physically. Both forms of linearity undermine performance.

When we began working with Marilyn Clark, a managing director of Salomon Smith Barney, she had almost no oscillation in her life. Clark, who is in her late 30s, runs the firm's Cleveland office. She is also the mother of three young children, and her husband is a high-powered executive in his own right. To all appearances, Clark lives an enviable life, and she was loath to complain about it. Yet her hectic lifestyle was exacting a cost, which became clear after some probing. In the mornings, temporarily fueled by coffee and a muffin, she was alert and energetic. By the afternoon, though, her energy sagged, and she got through the rest of the day on sheer willpower. At lunchtime, when she could have taken a few quiet moments to recover, she found that she couldn't say no to employees who lined up at her office seeking counsel and support. Between the demands of her job, her colleagues, and her family, she had almost no time for herself. Her frustration quietly grew.

We began our work with Clark by taking stock of her physical capacity. While she had been a passionate athlete as a teenager and an All-American lacrosse player in college, her fitness regimen for the past several years had been limited to occasional sit-ups before bedtime. As she learned more about the relationship between energy and high performance, Clark agreed that her first priority was to get back in shape. She wanted to feel better physically, and she knew from past experience that her mood would improve if she built regular workouts into her schedule.

Because old habits die hard, we helped Clark establish positive rituals to replace them. Part of the work was creating a supportive environment. The colleagues with whom Clark trained became a source of cheerleading—and even nagging—as she established a routine that would have previously seemed unthinkable. Clark committed to work out in a nearby gym three days a week, precisely at 1 PM. She also enlisted her husband to watch the kids so that she could get in a workout on Saturdays and Sundays.

Regular workouts have helped Clark create clear work-life boundaries and restored her sense of herself as an athlete. Now, rather than tumbling into an energy trough in the afternoons and reaching for a candy bar, Clark returns to the office from her workouts feeling reenergized and better able to focus. Physical stress has become a source not just of greater endurance but also of emotional and mental recovery; Clark finds that she can work fewer hours and get more done. And finally, because she no longer feels chronically overburdened, she believes that she has become a better boss. "My body feels reawakened," she says. "I'm much more relaxed, and the resentment I was feeling about all the demands on me is gone."

Clark has inspired other members of her firm to take out health club memberships. She and several colleagues are subsidizing employees who can't easily afford the cost. "We're not just talking to each other about business accolades and who is covering which account," she says. "Now it's also about whether we got our workouts in and how well we're recovering. We're sharing something healthy, and that has brought people together."

The corporate athlete doesn't build a strong physical foundation by exercise alone, of course. Good sleeping and eating rituals are integral to effective energy management. When we first met Rudy Borneo, the vice chairman of Macy's West, he complained of erratic energy levels, wide mood swings, and difficulty concentrating. He was also overweight. Like many executives—and most Americans—his eating habits were poor. He typically began his long, travel-crammed days by skipping breakfast—the equivalent of rolling to the start line of the Indianapolis 500 with a near-empty fuel tank. Lunch was catch-as-catch-can, and Borneo used sugary snacks to fight off his inevitable afternoon hunger pangs. These foods spiked his blood glucose levels, giving him a quick jolt of energy, but one that faded quickly. Dinner was often a rich, multi-course meal eaten late in the evening. Digesting that much food disturbed Borneo's sleep and left him feeling sluggish and out of sorts in the mornings.

Sound familiar?

As we did with Clark, we helped Borneo replace his bad habits with positive rituals, beginning with the way he ate. We explained that by eating lightly but often, he could sustain a steady level of energy. (For a fuller account of the foundational exercise, eating, and sleep routines, see "A Firm Foundation" at the end of this article.) Borneo now eats breakfast every day—typically a high-protein drink rather than coffee and a bagel. We also showed him research by chronobiologists suggesting that the body and mind need recovery every 90 to 120 minutes. Using that cycle as the basis for his eating schedule, he installed a refrigerator by his desk and began eating five or six small but nutritious meals a day and sipping water frequently. He also shifted the emphasis in his workouts to interval training, which increased his endurance and speed of recovery.

In addition to prompting weight loss and making him feel better, Borneo's nutritional and fitness rituals have had a dramatic effect on other aspects of his life. "I now exercise for my mind as much as for my body," he says. "At the age of 59, I have more energy than ever, and I can sustain it for a longer period of time. For me, the rituals are the holy grail. Using them to create balance has had an impact on every aspect of my life: staying more positive, handling difficult human resource issues, dealing with change, treating people better. I really do believe that when you learn to take care of yourself, you free up energy and enthusiasm to care more for others."

Emotional Capacity

The next building block of IPS is emotional capacity—the internal climate that supports peak performance. During our early research, we asked hundreds of athletes to describe how they felt when they were performing at their best. Invariably, they used words such as "calm," "challenged," "engaged," "focused," "optimistic," and "confident." As sprinter Marion Jones put it shortly after winning one of her gold medals at the Olympic Games in Sydney: "I'm out here having a ball. This is not a stressful time in my life. This is a very happy time." When we later asked the same question of law enforcement officers, military personnel, surgeons, and corporate executives, they used remarkably similar language to describe their Ideal Performance State.

Just as positive emotions ignite the energy that drives high performance, negative emotions—frustration, impatience, anger, fear, resentment, and sadness—drain energy. Over time, these feelings can be literally toxic, elevating heart rate and blood pressure, increasing muscle tension, constricting vision, and ultimately crippling performance. Anxious, fear ridden athletes are far more likely to choke in competition, for example, while anger and frustration sabotage their capacity for calm focus.

The impact of negative emotions on business performance is subtler but no less devastating. Alan, an executive at an investment company, travels frequently, overseeing a half-dozen offices around the country. His colleagues and subordinates, we learned, considered him to be a perfectionist and an often critical boss whose frustration and impatience sometimes boiled over into angry tirades. Our work focused on helping Alan find ways to manage his emotions more effectively. His anger, we explained, was a reactive emotion, a fight-or-flight response to situations he perceived as threatening. To manage more effectively, he needed to transform his inner experience of threat under stress into one of challenge.

A regular workout regimen built Alan's endurance and gave him a way to burn off tension. But because his fierce travel schedule often got in the way of his work-outs, we also helped him develop a precise five-step rit-ual to contain his negative emotions whenever they threatened to erupt. His initial challenge was to become more aware of signals from his body that he was on edge—physical tension, a racing heart, tightness in his chest. When he felt those sensations arise, his first step was to close his eyes and take several deep breaths. Next, he consciously relaxed the muscles in his face. Then, he made an effort to soften his voice and speak more slowly. After that, he tried to put himself in the shoes of the per-son who was the target of his anger—to imagine what he or she must be feeling. Finally, he focused on framing his response in positive language.

Instituting this ritual felt awkward to Alan at first, not unlike trying to learn a new golf swing. More than once he reverted to his old behavior. But within several weeks, the five-step drill had become automatic—a highly reliable way to short-circuit his reactivity. Numerous employees reported that he had become more reasonable, more approachable, and less scary. Alan himself says that he has become a far more effective manager.

Through our work with athletes, we have learned a number of other rituals that help to offset feelings of stress and restore positive energy. It's no coincidence, for example, that many athletes wear headphones as they prepare for competition. Music has powerful physiological and emotional effects. It can prompt a shift in mental activity from the rational left hemisphere of the brain to the more intuitive right hemisphere. It also provides a relief from obsessive thinking and worrying. Finally, music can be a means of directly regulating energy—raising it when the time comes to perform and lowering it when it is more appropriate to decompress.

Body language also influences emotions. In one well-known experiment, actors were asked to portray anger and then were subjected to numerous physiological tests, including heart rate, blood pressure, core temperature, galvanic skin response, and hormone levels. Next, the actors were exposed to a situation that made them genuinely angry, and the same measurements were taken. There were virtually no differences in the two profiles. Effective acting produces precisely the same physiology that real emotions do. All great athletes understand this instinctively. If they carry themselves confidently, they will eventually start to feel confident, even in highly stressful situations. That's why we train our corporate clients to "act as if"—consciously creating the look on the outside that they want to feel on the inside. "You are what you repeatedly do," said Aristotle. "Excellence is not a singular act but a habit."

Close relationships are perhaps the most powerful means for prompting positive emotions and effective recovery. Anyone who has enjoyed a happy family reunion or an evening with good friends knows the profound sense of safety and security that these relationships can induce. Such feelings are closely associated with the Ideal Performance State. Unfortunately, many of the corporate athletes we train believe that in order to perform up to expectations at work, they have no choice but to stint on their time with loved ones. We try to reframe the issue. By devoting more time to their most important relationships and setting clearer boundaries between work and home, we tell our clients, they will not only derive more satisfaction but will also get the recovery that they need to perform better at work.

Mental Capacity

The third level of the performance pyramid—the cognitive—is where most traditional performance-enhancement training is aimed. The usual approaches tend to focus on improving competencies by using techniques such as process reengineering and knowledge management or by learning to use more sophisticated technology. Our training aims to enhance our clients' cognitive capacities—most notably their focus, time management, and positive- and critical-thinking skills.

Focus simply means energy concentrated in the service of a particular goal. Anything that interferes with focus dissipates energy. Meditation, typically viewed as a spiritual practice, can serve as a highly practical means of training attention and promoting recovery. At this level, no guidance from a guru is required. A perfectly adequate meditation technique involves sitting quietly and breathing deeply, counting each exhalation, and starting over when you reach ten. Alternatively, you can choose a word to repeat each time you take a breath.

Practiced regularly, meditation quiets the mind, the emotions, and the body, promoting energy recovery. Numerous studies have shown, for example, that experienced meditators need considerably fewer hours of sleep than nonmeditators. Meditation and other noncognitive disciplines can also slow brain wave activity and stimulate a shift in mental activity from the left hemisphere of the brain to the right. Have you ever suddenly found the solution to a vexing problem while doing something "mindless" such as jogging, working in the garden, or singing in the shower? That's the left-brain, right-brain shift at work—the fruit of mental oscillation.

Much of our training at this level focuses on helping corporate athletes to consciously manage their time and energy. By alternating periods of stress with renewal, they learn to align their work with the body's need for breaks every 90 to 120 minutes. This can be challenging for compulsive corporate achievers. Jeffrey Sklar, 39, managing director for institutional sales at the New York investment firm Gruntal & Company, had long been accustomed to topping his competitors by brute force— pushing harder and more relentlessly than anyone else. With our help, he built a set of rituals that ensured regular recovery and also enabled him to perform at a higher level while spending fewer hours at work.

Once in the morning and again in the afternoon, Sklar retreats from the frenetic trading floor to a quiet office, where he spends 15 minutes doing deep-breathing exercises. At lunch, he leaves the office—something he once would have found unthinkable—and walks outdoors for at least 15 minutes. He also works out five or six times a week after work. At home, he and his wife, Sherry, a busy executive herself, made a pact never to talk business after 8 PM. They also swore off work on the weekends, and they have stuck to their vow for nearly two years. During each of those years, Sklar's earnings have increased by more than 65%.

For Jim Connor, the president and CEO of FootJoy, reprioritizing his time became a way not just to manage his energy better but to create more balance in his life and to revive his sense of passion. Connor had come to us saying that he felt stuck in a deep rut. "My feelings were muted so I could deal with the emotional pain of life," he explains. "I had smoothed out all the vicissitudes in my life to such an extent that oscillation was prohibited. I was not feeling life but repetitively performing it."

Connor had imposed on himself the stricture that he be the first person to arrive at the office each day and the last to leave. In reality, he acknowledged, no one would object if he arrived a little later or left a little earlier a couple of days a week. He realized it also made sense for him to spend one or two days a week working at a satellite plant 45 minutes nearer to his home than his main office. Doing so could boost morale at the second plant while cutting 90 minutes from his commute.

Immediately after working with us, Connor arranged to have an office cleared out at the satellite factory. He now spends at least one full day a week there, prompting a number of people at that office to comment to him about his increased availability. He began taking a golf lesson one morning a week, which also allowed for a more relaxed drive to his main office, since he commutes there after rush hour on golf days. In addition, he instituted a monthly getaway routine with his wife. In the evenings, he often leaves his office earlier in order to spend more time with his family.

Connor has also meticulously built recovery into his workdays. "What a difference these fruit and water breaks make," he says. "I set my alarm watch for 90 minutes to prevent relapses, but I'm instinctively incorporating this routine into my life and love it. I'm far more productive as a result, and the quality of my thought process is measurably improved. I'm also doing more on the big things at work and not getting bogged down in detail. I'm pausing more to think and to take time out."

Rituals that encourage positive thinking also increase the likelihood of accessing the Ideal Performance State. Once again, our work with top athletes has taught us the power of creating specific mental rituals to sustain positive energy. Jack Nicklaus, one of the greatest pressure performers in the history of golf, seems to have an intuitive understanding of the importance of both oscillation and rituals. "I've developed a regimen that allows me to move from peaks of concentration into valleys of relaxation and back again as necessary," he wrote in *Golf Digest*. "My focus begins to sharpen as I walk onto the tee and steadily intensifies . . . until I hit [my drive]. . . . I descend into a valley as I leave the tee, either through casual conversation with a fellow competitor or by letting my mind dwell on whatever happens into it."

Visualization is another ritual that produces positive energy and has palpable performance results. For example, Earl Woods taught his son Tiger—Nicklaus's heir apparent—to form a mental image of the ball rolling into the hole before each shot. The exercise does more than produce a vague feeling of optimism and well-being. Neuroscientist Ian Robertson of Trinity College, Dublin, author of *Mind Sculpture*, has found that visualization can literally reprogram the neural circuitry of the brain, directly improving performance. It is hard to imagine a better illustration than diver Laura Wilkinson. Six months before the summer Olympics in Sydney, Wilkinson broke three toes on her right foot while training. Unable to go in the water because of her cast, she instead spent hours a day on the diving platform, visualizing each of her dives. With only a few weeks to actually practice before the Olympics, she pulled off a huge upset, winning the gold medal on the ten-meter platform.

Visualization works just as well in the office. Sherry Sklar has a ritual to prepare for any significant event in her work life. "I always take time to sit down in advance in a quiet place and think about what I really want from the meeting," she says. "Then I visualize myself achieving the outcome I'm after." In effect, Sklar is building mental muscles—increasing her strength, endurance, and flexibility. By doing so, she decreases the likelihood that she will be distracted by negative thoughts under pressure. "It has made me much more relaxed and confident when I go into presentations," she says.

Spiritual Capacity

Most executives are wary of addressing the spiritual level of the performance pyramid in business settings, and understandably so. The word "spiritual" prompts conflicting emotions and doesn't seem immediately relevant to high performance. So let's be clear: by spiritual capacity, we simply mean the energy that is unleashed by tapping into one's deepest values and defining a strong sense of purpose. This capacity, we have found, serves as sustenance in the face of adversity and as a powerful source of motivation, focus, determination, and resilience.

Consider the case of Ann, a high-level executive at a large cosmetics company. For much of her adult life, she has tried unsuccessfully to quit smoking, blaming her failures on a lack of self-discipline. Smoking took a visible toll on her health and her productivity at work—decreased endurance from shortness of breath, more sick days than her colleagues, and nicotine cravings that distracted her during long meetings.

Four years ago, when Ann became pregnant, she was able to quit immediately and didn't touch a cigarette until the day her child was born, when she began smoking again. A year later, Ann became pregnant for a second time, and again she stopped smoking, with virtually no symptoms of withdrawal. True to her pattern, she resumed smoking when her child was born. "I don't understand it," she told us plaintively.

We offered a simple explanation. As long as Ann was able to connect the impact of smoking to a deeper purpose—the health of her unborn child—quitting was easy. She was able to make what we call a "values-based adaptation." But without a strong connection to a deeper sense of purpose, she went back to smoking—an expedient adaptation that served her short-term interests. Smoking was a sensory pleasure for Ann, as well as a way to allay her anxiety and manage social stress. Understanding cognitively that it was unhealthy, feeling guilty about it on an emotional level, and even experiencing its negative effects physically were all insufficient motivations to change her behavior. To succeed, Ann needed a more sustaining source of motivation.

Making such a connection, we have found, requires regularly stepping off the endless treadmill of deadlines and obligations to take time for reflection. The inclination for busy executives is to live in a perpetual state of triage, doing whatever seems most immediately pressing while losing sight of any bigger picture. Rituals that give people the opportunity to pause and look inside include meditation, journal writing, prayer, and service to others. Each of these activities can also serve as a source of recovery—a way to break the linearity of relentless goal-oriented activity.

Taking the time to connect to one's deepest values can be extremely rewarding. It can also be painful, as a client we'll call Richard discovered. Richard is a stockbroker who works in New York City and lives in a distant suburb, where his wife stays at home with their three young children. Between his long commute and his long hours, Richard spent little time with his family. Like so many of our clients, he typically left home before his children woke up and returned around 7:30 in the evening, feeling exhausted and in no mood to talk to anyone. He wasn't happy with his situation, but he saw no easy solution. In time, his unhappiness began to affect his work, which made him even more negative when he got home at night. It was a vicious cycle.

One evening while driving home from work, Richard found himself brooding about his life. Suddenly, he felt so overcome by emotion that he stopped his car at a park ten blocks from home to collect himself. To his astonishment, he began to weep. He felt consumed with grief about his life and filled with longing for his family. After ten minutes, all Richard wanted to do was get home and hug his wife and children. Accustomed to giving their dad a wide berth at the end of the day, his kids were understandably bewildered when he walked in that evening with tears streaming down his face and wrapped them all in hugs. When his wife arrived on the scene, her first thought was that he'd been fired.

The next day, Richard again felt oddly compelled to stop at the park near his house. Sure enough, the tears returned and so did the longing. Once again, he rushed home to his family. During the subsequent two years, Richard was able to count on one hand the number of times that he failed to stop at the same location for at least ten minutes. The rush of emotion subsided over time, but his sense that he was affirming what mattered most in his life remained as strong as ever.

Richard had stumbled into a ritual that allowed him both to disengage from work and to tap into a profound source of purpose and meaning—his family. In that context, going home ceased to be a burden after a long day and became instead a source of recovery and renewal. In turn, Richard's distraction at work diminished, and he became more focused, positive, and productive—so much so that he was able to cut down on his hours. On a practical level, he created a better balance between stress and recovery. Finally, by tapping into a deeper sense of purpose, he found a powerful new source of energy for both his work and his family.

IN A CORPORATE ENVIRONMENT that is changing at warp speed, performing consistently at high levels is more difficult and more necessary than ever. Narrow interventions simply aren't sufficient anymore. Companies can't afford to address their employees' cognitive capacities while ignoring their physical, emotional, and spiritual well-being. On the playing field or in the boardroom, high performance depends as much on how people renew and recover energy as on how they expend it, on how they manage their lives as much as on how they manage their work. When people feel strong and resilient—physically, mentally, emotionally, and spiritually—they perform better, with more passion, for longer. They win, their families win, and the corporations that employ them win.

A Firm Foundation

HERE ARE OUR BASIC STRATEGIES for renewing energy at the physical level. Some of them are so familiar they've become background noise, easy to ignore. That's why we're repeating them. If any of these strategies aren't part of your life now, their absence may help account for fatigue, irritability, lack of emotional resilience, difficulty concentrating, and even a flagging sense of purpose.

1. **Actually do all those healthy things you know you ought to do.** Eat five or six small meals a day; people who eat just one or two meals a day with long periods in between force their bodies into a conservation mode, which translates into slower metabolism. Always eat breakfast: eating first thing in the morning sends your body the signal that it need not slow metabolism to conserve energy. Eat a balanced diet. Despite all the con-

flicting nutritional research, overwhelming evidence suggests that a healthy dietary ratio is 50% to 60% complex carbohydrates, 25% to 35% protein, and 20% to 25% fat. Dramatically reduce simple sugars. In addition to representing empty calories, sugar causes energy-depleting spikes in blood glucose levels. Drink four to five 12-ounce glasses of water daily, even if you don't feel thirsty. As much as half the population walks around with mild chronic dehydration. And finally, on the "you know you should" list: get physically active. We strongly recommend three to four 20- to 30-minute cardiovascular workouts a week, including at least two sessions of intervals—short bursts of intense exertion followed by brief recovery periods.

2. **Go to bed early and wake up early.** Night owls have a much more difficult time dealing with the demands of today's business world, because typically, they still have to get up with the early birds. They're often groggy and unfocused in the mornings, dependent on caffeine and sugary snacks to keep up their energy. You can establish new sleep rituals. Biological clocks are not fixed in our genes.

3. **Maintain a consistent bedtime and wake-up time.** As important of the number of hours you sleep (ideally seven to eight) is the consistency of the recovery wave you create. Regular sleep cycles help regulate your other biological clocks and increase the likelihood that the sleep you get will be deep and restful.

4. **Seek recovery every 90 to 120 minutes.** Chronobiologists have found that the body's hormone, glucose, and blood pressure levels drop every 90 minutes or so. By failing to seek recovery and overriding the body's natural stress-rest cycles, overall capacity is compromised. As

we've learned from athletes, even short, focused breaks can promote significant recovery. We suggest five sources of restoration: eat something, hydrate, move physically, change channels mentally, and change channels emotionally.

5. **Do at least two weight-training workouts a week.** No form of exercise more powerfully turns back the markers of age than weight training. It increases strength, retards osteoporosis, speeds up metabolism, enhances mobility, improves posture, and dramatically increases energy.

Originally published in January 2001
Reprint R0101H

Crucibles of Leadership

WARREN G. BENNIS AND
ROBERT J. THOMAS

Executive Summary

WHAT MAKES A GREAT LEADER? Why do some people appear to know instinctively how to inspire employees—bringing out their confidence, loyalty, and dedication—while others flounder again and again? No simple formula can explain how great leaders come to be, but Bennis and Thomas believe it has something to do with the ways people handle adversity. The authors' recent research suggests that one of the most reliable indicators and predictors of true leadership is the ability to learn from even the most negative experiences. An extraordinary leader is a kind of phoenix rising from the ashes of adversity stronger and more committed than ever.

In interviewing more than 40 leaders in business and the public sector over the past three years, the authors discovered that all of them—young and old alike—had endured intense, often traumatic, experiences that transformed them and became the source of their distinctive leadership abilities.

Bennis and Thomas call these shaping experiences "crucibles," after the vessels medieval alchemists used in their attempts to turn base metals into gold. For the interviewees, their crucibles were the points at which they were forced to question who they were and what was important to them. These experiences made them stronger and more confident and changed their sense of purpose in some fundamental way.

Through a variety of examples, the authors explore the idea of the crucible in detail. They also reveal that great leaders possess four essential skills, the most critical of which is "adaptive capacity"—an almost magical ability to transcend adversity and emerge stronger than before.

As LIFELONG STUDENTS of leadership, we are fascinated with the notion of what makes a leader. Why is it that certain people seem to naturally inspire confidence, loyalty, and hard work, while others (who may have just as much vision and smarts) stumble, again and again? It's a timeless question, and there's no simple answer. But we have come to believe it has something to do with the different ways that people deal with adversity. Indeed, our recent research has led us to conclude that one of the most reliable indicators and predictors of true leadership is an individual's ability to find meaning in negative events and to learn from even the most trying circumstances. Put another way, the skills required to conquer adversity and emerge stronger and more committed than ever are the same ones that make for extraordinary leaders.

Take Sidney Harman. Thirty-four years ago, the then-48-year-old businessman was holding down two executive positions. He was the chief executive of Harman Kardon (now Harman International), the audio components company he had cofounded, and he was serving as president of Friends World College, now Friends World Program, an experimental Quaker school on Long Island whose essential philosophy is that students, not their teachers, are responsible for their education. Juggling the two jobs, Harman was living what he calls a "bifurcated life," changing clothes in his car and eating lunch as he drove between Harman Kardon offices and plants and the Friends World campus. One day while at the college, he was told his company's factory in Bolivar, Tennessee, was having a crisis.

He immediately rushed to the Bolivar factory, a facility that was, as Harman now recalls, "raw, ugly, and, in many ways, demeaning." The problem, he found, had erupted in the polish and buff department, where a crew of a dozen workers, mostly African-Americans, did the dull, hard work of polishing mirrors and other parts, often under unhealthy conditions. The men on the night shift were supposed to get a coffee break at 10 PM. When the buzzer that announced the workers' break went on the fritz, management arbitrarily decided to postpone the break for ten minutes, when another buzzer was scheduled to sound. But one worker, "an old black man with an almost biblical name, Noah B. Cross," had "an epiphany," as Harman describes it. "He said, literally, to his fellow workers, 'I don't work for no buzzer. The buzzer works for me. It's my job to tell me when it's ten o'clock. I got me a watch. I'm not waiting another ten minutes. I'm going on my coffee break.' And all 12 guys took their coffee break, and, of course, all hell broke loose."

The worker's principled rebellion—his refusal to be cowed by management's senseless rule—was, in turn, a revelation to Harman: "The technology is there to serve the men, not the reverse," he remembers realizing. "I suddenly had this awakening that everything I was doing at the college had appropriate applications in business." In the ensuing years, Harman revamped the factory and its workings, turning it into a kind of campus—offering classes on the premises, including piano lessons, and encouraging the workers to take most of the responsibility for running their workplace. Further, he created an environment where dissent was not only tolerated but also encouraged. The plant's lively independent newspaper, the *Bolivar Mirror*, gave workers a creative and emotional outlet—and they enthusiastically skewered Harman in its pages.

Harman had, unexpectedly, become a pioneer of participative management, a movement that continues to influence the shape of workplaces around the world. The concept wasn't a grand idea conceived in the CEO's office and imposed on the plant, Harman says. It grew organically out of his going down to Bolivar to, in his words, "put out this fire." Harman's transformation was, above all, a creative one. He had connected two seemingly unrelated ideas and created a radically different approach to management that recognized both the economic and humane benefits of a more collegial workplace. Harman went on to accomplish far more during his career. In addition to founding Harman International, he served as the deputy secretary of commerce under Jimmy Carter. But he always looked back on the incident in Bolivar as the formative event in his professional life, the moment he came into his own as a leader.

The details of Harman's story are unique, but their significance is not. In interviewing more than 40 top leaders in business and the public sector over the past three years, we were surprised to find that all of them—young and old—were able to point to intense, often traumatic, always unplanned experiences that had transformed them and had become the sources of their distinctive leadership abilities.

We came to call the experiences that shape leaders "crucibles," after the vessels medieval alchemists used in their attempts to turn base metals into gold. For the leaders we interviewed, the crucible experience was a trial and a test, a point of deep self-reflection that forced them to question who they were and what mattered to them. It required them to examine their values, question their assumptions, hone their judgment. And, invariably, they emerged from the crucible stronger and more sure of themselves and their purpose—changed in some fundamental way.

Leadership crucibles can take many forms. Some are violent, life-threatening events. Others are more prosaic episodes of self-doubt. But whatever the crucible's nature, the people we spoke with were able, like Harman, to create a narrative around it, a story of how they were challenged, met the challenge, and became better leaders. As we studied these stories, we found that they not only told us how individual leaders are shaped but also pointed to some characteristics that seem common to all leaders—characteristics that were formed, or at least exposed, in the crucible.

Learning from Difference

A crucible is, by definition, a transformative experience through which an individual comes to a new or an altered sense of identity. It is perhaps not surprising then that one of the most common types of crucibles we

documented involves the experience of prejudice. Being
a victim of prejudice is particularly traumatic because it
forces an individual to confront a distorted picture of
him- or herself, and it often unleashes profound feelings
of anger, bewilderment, and even withdrawal. For all its
trauma, however, the experience of prejudice is for some
a clarifying event. Through it, they gain a clearer vision
of who they are, the role they play, and their place in the
world.

Consider, for example, Liz Altman, now a Motorola
vice president, who was transformed by the year she
spent at a Sony camcorder factory in rural Japan, where
she faced both estrangement and sexism. It was, says
Altman, "by far, the hardest thing I've ever done." The
foreign culture—particularly its emphasis on groups
over individuals—was both a shock and a challenge to a
young American woman. It wasn't just that she felt
lonely in an alien world. She had to face the daunting
prospect of carving out a place for herself as the only
woman engineer in a plant, and nation, where women
usually serve as low-level assistants and clerks known as
"office ladies."

Another woman who had come to Japan under similar
circumstances had warned Altman that the only way to
win the men's respect was to avoid becoming allied with
the office ladies. But on her very first morning, when the
bell rang for a coffee break, the men headed in one direction and the women in another—and the women saved
her a place at their table, while the men ignored her.
Instinct told Altman to ignore the warning rather than
insult the women by rebuffing their invitation.

Over the next few days, she continued to join the
women during breaks, a choice that gave her a comfortable haven from which to observe the unfamiliar office

culture. But it didn't take her long to notice that some of
the men spent the break at their desks reading maga-
zines, and Altman determined that she could do the
same on occasion. Finally, after paying close attention to
the conversations around her, she learned that several of
the men were interested in mountain biking. Because
Altman wanted to buy a mountain bike, she approached
them for advice. Thus, over time, she established herself
as something of a free agent, sometimes sitting with the
women and other times engaging with the men.

And as it happened, one of the women she'd sat with
on her very first day, the department secretary, was mar-
ried to one of the engineers. The secretary took it upon
herself to include Altman in social gatherings, a turn of
events that probably wouldn't have occurred if Altman
had alienated her female coworkers on that first day.
"Had I just gone to try to break in with [the men] and not
had her as an ally, it would never have happened," she
says.

Looking back, Altman believes the experience greatly
helped her gain a clearer sense of her personal strengths
and capabilities, preparing her for other difficult situations. Her tenure in Japan taught her to observe closely
and to avoid jumping to conclusions based on cultural
assumptions—invaluable skills in her current position at
Motorola, where she leads efforts to smooth alliances
with other corporate cultures, including those of
Motorola's different regional operations.

Altman has come to believe that she wouldn't have
been as able to do the Motorola job if she hadn't lived in
a foreign country and experienced the dissonance of cultures: ". . . even if you're sitting in the same room, osten-
sibly agreeing . . . unless you understand the frame of
reference, you're probably missing a bunch of what's

going on." Altman also credits her crucible with building her confidence—she feels that she can cope with just about anything that comes her way.

People can feel the stigma of cultural differences much closer to home, as well. Muriel ("Mickie") Siebert, the first woman to own a seat on the New York Stock Exchange, found her crucible on the Wall Street of the 1950s and 1960s, an arena so sexist that she couldn't get a job as a stockbroker until she took her first name off her résumé and substituted a genderless initial. Other than the secretaries and the occasional analyst, women were few and far between. That she was Jewish was another strike against her at a time, she points out, when most of big business was "not nice" to either women or Jews. But Siebert wasn't broken or defeated. Instead, she emerged stronger, more focused, and more determined to change the status quo that excluded her.

When we interviewed Siebert, she described her way of addressing anti-Semitism—a technique that quieted the offensive comments of her peers without destroying the relationships she needed to do her job effectively. According to Siebert, at the time it was part of doing business to have a few drinks at lunch. She remembers, "Give somebody a couple of drinks, and they would talk about the Jews." She had a greeting card she used for those occasions that went like this:

> *Roses are reddish,*
> *Violets are bluish,*
> *In case you don't know,*
> *I am Jewish.*

Siebert would have the card hand-delivered to the person who had made the anti-Semitic remarks, and on the card she had written, "Enjoyed lunch." As she recounts, "They got that card in the afternoon, and I never had to take any of that nonsense again. And I never embarrassed anyone, either." It was because she was unable to get credit for the business she was bringing in at any of the large Wall Street firms that she bought a seat on the New York Stock Exchange and started working for herself.

In subsequent years, she went on to found Muriel Siebert & Company (now Siebert Financial Corporation) and has dedicated herself to helping other people avoid some of the difficulties she faced as a young professional. A prominent advocate for women in business and a leader in developing financial products directed at women, she's also devoted to educating children about financial opportunities and responsibility.

We didn't interview lawyer and presidential adviser Vernon Jordan for this article, but he, too, offers a powerful reminder of how prejudice can prove transformational rather than debilitating. In *Vernon Can Read! A Memoir* (Public Affairs, 2001), Jordan describes the vicious baiting he was subjected to as a young man. The man who treated him in this offensive way was his employer, Robert F. Maddox. Jordan served the racist former mayor of Atlanta at dinner, in a white jacket, with a napkin over his arm. He also functioned as Maddox's chauffeur. Whenever Maddox could, he would derisively announce, "Vernon can read!" as if the literacy of a young African-American were a source of wonderment.

Subjected to this type of abuse, a lesser man might have allowed Maddox to destroy him. But in his memoir, Jordan gives his own interpretation of Maddox's sadistic heckling, a tale that empowered Jordan instead of embittering him. When he looked at Maddox through the rearview mirror, Jordan did not see a powerful member of Georgia's ruling class. He saw a desperate anachronism, a person who lashed out because he knew his time was up. As Jordan writes about Maddox, "His half-mocking, half-serious comments about my education were the death rattle of his culture. When he saw that I was . . . crafting a life for myself that would make me a man in . . . ways he thought of as being a man, he was deeply unnerved."

Maddox's cruelty was the crucible that, consciously or not, Jordan imbued with redemptive meaning. Instead of lashing out or being paralyzed with hatred, Jordan saw the fall of the Old South and imagined his own future freed of the historical shackles of racism. His ability to organize meaning around a potential crisis turned it into the crucible around which his leadership was forged.

Prevailing over Darkness

Some crucible experiences illuminate a hidden and suppressed area of the soul. These are often among the harshest of crucibles, involving, for instance, episodes of illness or violence. In the case of Sidney Rittenberg, now 79, the crucible took the form of 16 years of unjust imprisonment, in solitary confinement, in Communist China. In 1949 Rittenberg was initially jailed, without explanation, by former friends in Chairman Mao Zedong's government and spent his first year in total darkness when he wasn't being interrogated. (Rittenberg later learned that his arrest came at the behest of Communist Party officials in Moscow, who had wrongly identified him as a CIA agent.) Thrown into jail, confined to a tiny, pitch-dark cell, Rittenberg did not rail or panic. Instead, within minutes, he remembered a stanza of verse, four lines recited to him when he was a small child:

They drew a circle that shut me out,
Heretic, rebel, a thing to flout.
But love and I had the wit to win,
We drew a circle that took them in!

That bit of verse (adapted from "Outwitted," a poem by Edwin Markham) was the key to Rittenberg's survival. "My God," he thought, "there's my strategy." He drew the prison guards into his circle, developing relationships that would help him adapt to his confinement. Fluent in Chinese, he persuaded the guards to deliver him books and, eventually, provide a candle so that he could read. He also decided, after his first year, to devote himself to improving his mind—making it more scientific, more pure, and more dedicated to socialism. He believed that if he raised his consciousness, his captors would understand him better. And when, over time, the years in the dark began to take an intellectual toll on him and he found his reason faltering, he could still summon fairy tales and childhood stories such as *The Little Engine That Could* and take comfort from their simple messages.

By contrast, many of Rittenberg's fellow prisoners either lashed out in anger or withdrew. "They tended to go up the wall. . . . They couldn't make it. And I think the reason was that they didn't understand . . . that happiness . . . is not a function of your circumstances; it's a function of your outlook on life."

Rittenberg's commitment to his ideals continued upon his release. His cell door opened suddenly in 1955, after his first six-year term in prison. He recounts, "Here was a representative of the central government telling me that I had been wronged, that the government was making a formal apology to me . . . and that they would do everything possible to make restitution." When his captors offered him money to start a new life in the United States or to travel in Europe, Rittenberg declined, choosing instead to stay in China and continue his work for the Communist Party.

And even after a second arrest, which put him into solitary confinement for ten years as retaliation for his support of open democracy during the Cultural Revolution, Rittenberg did not allow his spirit to be broken. Instead, he used his time in prison as an opportunity to question his belief system—in particular, his commitment to Marxism and Chairman Mao. "In that sense, prison emancipated me," he says.

Rittenberg studied, read, wrote, and thought, and he learned something about himself in the process: "I realized I had this great fear of being a turncoat, which . . . was so powerful that it prevented me from even looking at [my assumptions]. . . . Even to question was an act of betrayal. After I got out . . . the scales fell away from my eyes and I understood that . . . the basic doctrine of arriving at democracy through dictatorship was wrong."

What's more, Rittenberg emerged from prison certain that absolutely nothing in his professional life could break him and went on to start a company with his wife. Rittenberg Associates is a consulting firm dedicated to developing business ties between the United States and China. Today, Rittenberg is as committed to his ideals— if not to his view of the best way to get there—as he was 50 years ago, when he was so severely tested.

Meeting Great Expectations

Fortunately, not all crucible experiences are traumatic. In fact, they can involve a positive, if deeply challenging, experience such as having a demanding boss or mentor. Judge Nathaniel R. Jones of the U.S. Court of Appeals for the Sixth Circuit, for instance, attributes much of his success to his interaction with a splendid mentor. That mentor was J. Maynard Dickerson, a successful attorney—the first black city prosecutor in the United States—and editor of a local African-American newspaper.

Dickerson influenced Jones at many levels. For instance, the older man brought Jones behind the scenes to witness firsthand the great civil rights struggle of the 1950s, inviting him to sit in on conversations with activists like Thurgood Marshall, Walter White, Roy Wilkins, and Robert C. Weaver. Says Jones, "I was struck by their resolve, their humor . . . and their determination not to let the system define them. Rather than just feel beaten down, they turned it around." The experience no doubt influenced the many important opinions Judge Jones has written in regard to civil rights.

Dickerson was both model and coach. His lessons covered every aspect of Jones's intellectual growth and presentation of self, including schooling in what we now call "emotional intelligence." Dickerson set the highest standards for Jones, especially in the area of communication skills—a facility we've found essential to leadership. Dickerson edited Jones's early attempts at writing a sports column with respectful ruthlessness, in red ink, as Jones remembers to this day—marking up the copy so that it looked, as Jones says, "like something chickens had a fight over." But Dickerson also took the time to explain every single mistake and why it mattered.

His mentor also expected the teenage Jones to speak correctly at all times and would hiss discreetly in his direction if he stumbled. Great expectations are evidence of great respect, and as Jones learned all the complex, often subtle lessons of how to succeed, he was motivated in no small measure by his desire not to disappoint the man he still calls "Mr. Dickerson." Dickerson gave Jones the kind of intensive mentoring that was tantamount to grooming him for a kind of professional and moral succession—and Jones has indeed become an instrument for the profound societal change for which Dickerson fought so courageously as well. Jones found life-changing meaning in the attention Dickerson paid to him—attention fueled by a conviction that he, too, though only a teenager, had a vital role to play in society and an important destiny.

Another story of a powerful mentor came to us from Michael Klein, a young man who made millions in Southern California real estate while still in his teens, only to lose it by the time he turned 20 and then go on to start several other businesses. His mentor was his grandfather Max S. Klein, who created the paint-by-numbers fad that swept the United States in the 1950s and 1960s. Klein was only four or five years old when his grandfather approached him and offered to share his business expertise. Over the years, Michael Klein's grandfather taught him to learn from and to cope with change, and the two spoke by phone for an hour every day until shortly before Max Klein's death.

The Essentials of Leadership

In our interviews, we heard many other stories of crucible experiences. Take Jack Coleman, 78-year-old former president of Haverford College in Pennsylvania. He told us of one day, during the Vietnam War, when he heard that a group of students was planning to pull down the American flag and burn it—and that former members of the school's football team were going to make sure the students didn't succeed. Seemingly out of nowhere, Coleman had the idea to preempt the violence by suggesting that the protesting students take down the flag, wash it, and then put it back up—a crucible moment that even now elicits tremendous emotion in Coleman as he describes that day.

There's also Common Cause founder John W. Gardner, who died earlier this year at 89. He identified his arduous training as a Marine during World War II as the crucible in which his leadership abilities emerged. Architect Frank Gehry spoke of the biases he experienced as a Jew in college. Jeff Wilke, a general manager at a major manufacturer, told us of the day he learned that an employee had been killed in his plant—an experience that taught him that leadership was about much more than making quarterly numbers.

So, what allowed these people to not only cope with these difficult situations but also learn from them? We believe that great leaders possess four essential skills, and, we were surprised to learn, these happen to be the same skills that allow a person to find meaning in what could be a debilitating experience. First is the ability to engage others in shared meaning. Consider Sidney Harman, who dived into a chaotic work environment to mobilize employees around an entirely new approach to management. Second is a distinctive and compelling voice. Look at Jack Coleman's ability to defuse a potentially violent situation with only his words. Third is a sense of integrity (including a strong set of values). Here, we point again to Coleman, whose values prevailed even during the emotionally charged clash between peace demonstrators and the angry (and strong) former football team members.

But by far the most critical skill of the four is what we call "adaptive capacity." This is, in essence, applied creativity—an almost magical ability to transcend adversity, with all its attendant stresses, and to emerge stronger than before. It's composed of two primary qualities: the ability to grasp context, and hardiness. The ability to grasp context implies an ability to weigh a welter of factors, ranging from how very different groups of people will interpret a gesture to being able to put a situation in perspective. Without this, leaders are utterly lost, because they cannot connect with their constituents. M. Douglas Ivester, who succeeded Roberto Goizueta at Coca-Cola, exhibited a woeful inability to grasp context, lasting just 28 months on the job. For example, he demoted his highest-ranked African-American employee even as the company was losing a $200 million class-action suit brought by black employees—and this in Atlanta, a city with a powerful African-American majority. Contrast Ivester with Vernon Jordan. Jordan realized his boss's time was up—not just his time in power, but the era that formed him. And so Jordan was able to see past the insults and recognize his boss's bitterness for what it was—desperate lashing out.

Hardiness is just what it sounds like—the perseverance and toughness that enable people to emerge from devastating circumstances without losing hope. Look at Michael Klein, who experienced failure but didn't let it defeat him. He found himself with a single asset—a tiny software company he'd acquired. Klein built it into Transoft Networks, which Hewlett-Packard acquired in 1999. Consider, too, Mickie Siebert, who used her sense of humor to curtail offensive conversations. Or Sidney Rittenberg's strength during his imprisonment. He drew on his personal memories and inner strength to emerge from his lengthy prison term without bitterness.

It is the combination of hardiness and ability to grasp context that, above all, allows a person to not only survive an ordeal, but to learn from it, and to emerge stronger, more engaged, and more committed than ever. These attributes allow leaders to grow from their crucibles, instead of being destroyed by them—to find opportunity where others might find only despair. This is the stuff of true leadership.

Geeks and Geezers

WE DIDN'T SET OUT TO LEARN about crucibles. Our research for this article and for our new book, *Geeks and Geezers*, was actually designed to uncover the ways that era influences a leader's motivation and aspirations. We interviewed 43 of today's top leaders in business and the public sector, limiting our subjects to people born in or before 1925, or in or after 1970. To our delight, we learned a lot about how age and era affect leadership style.

Our geeks and geezers (the affectionate shorthand we eventually used to describe the two groups) had very different ideas about paying your dues, work-life balance, the role of heroes, and more. But they also shared some striking similarities—among them a love of learning and strong sense of values. Most intriguing, though, both our geeks and our geezers told us again and again how certain experiences inspired them, shaped them, and, indeed, taught them to lead. And so, as the best research often does, our work turned out to be even more interesting than we thought it would be. We continued to explore the influences of era—our findings are described in our book—but at the same time we probed for stories of these crucible experiences. These are the stories we share with you here.

Reinvention in the Extreme: The Power of Neoteny

ALL OF OUR INTERVIEW SUBJECTS described their crucibles as opportunities for reinvention—for taking stock of their lives and finding meaning in circumstances many people would see as daunting and potentially incapacitating. In the extreme, this capacity for reinvention comes to resemble eternal youth—a kind of vigor, openness, and an enduring capacity for wonder that is the antithesis of stereotyped old age.

We borrowed a term from biology—"neoteny," which, according to the *American Heritage Dictionary*, means "retention of juvenile characteristics in the adults of a species"—to describe this quality, this delight in lifelong learning, which every leader we interviewed displayed, regardless of age. To a person, they were full of energy, curiosity, and confidence that the world is a place of wonders spread before them like an endless feast.

Robert Galvin, former Motorola chairman now in his late 70s, spends his weekends windsurfing. Arthur Levitt, Jr., former SEC chairman who turned 71 this year, is an avid Outward Bound trekker. And architect Frank Gehry is now a 72-year-old ice hockey player. But it's not only an affinity for physical activity that characterizes neoteny—it's an appetite for learning and self-development, a curiosity and passion for life.

To understand why this quality is so powerful in a leader, it might help to take a quick look at the scientific principle behind it—neoteny as an evolutionary engine. It is the winning, puppyish quality of certain ancient wolves that allowed them to evolve into dogs. Over thousands of years, humans favored wolves that were the friendliest, most approachable, and most curious. Naturally, people were most drawn to the wolves least likely to attack without warning, that readily locked eyes with them, and that seemed almost human in their eager response to people; the ones, in short, that stayed the most like puppies. Like human infants, they have certain physical qualities that elicit a nurturing response in human adults.

When infants see an adult, they often respond with a smile that begins small and slowly grows into a radiant grin that makes the adult feel at center of the universe. Recent studies of bonding indicate that nursing and other intimate interactions with an infant cause the mother's system to be flooded with oxytocin, a calming, feel-good hormone that is a powerful antidote to cortisol, the hormone produced by stress. Oxytocin appears to be the glue that produces bonding. And the baby's distinctive look and behaviors cause oxytocin to be released in the fortunate adult. That appearance—the one that pulls an involuntary "aaah" out of us whenever we see a baby—and those oxytocin-inducing behaviors allow infants to recruit adults to be their nurturers, essential if such vulnerable and incompletely developed creatures are to survive.

The power of neoteny to recruit protectors and nurturers was vividly illustrated in the former Soviet Union. Forty years ago, a Soviet scientist decided to start breeding silver foxes for neoteny at a Siberian fur farm. The goal was to create a tamer fox that would go with less fuss to slaughter than the typical silver fox. Only the least aggressive, most approachable animals were bred.

The experiment continued for 40 years, and today, after 35 generations, the farm is home to a breed of tame foxes that look and act more like juvenile foxes and even dogs than like their wild forebears. The physical changes in the animals are remarkable (some have floppy, dog-like ears), but what is truly stunning is the change neoteny has wrought in the human response to them. Instead of taking advantage of the fact that these neotenic animals don't snap and snarl on the way to their deaths, their human keepers appear to have been recruited by their newly cute and endearing charges. The keepers and the foxes appear to have formed close bonds, so close that the keepers are trying to find ways to save the animals from slaughter.

Originally published in September 2002
Reprint R0209B

About the Contributors

CHRIS ARGYRIS is the James B. Conant Professor emeritus at the Harvard graduate schools of business and education. His most recent book is *Flawed Advice*, published in 2000. Previous articles in HBR include "Empowerment: The Emperor's New Clothes," "Skilled Incompetence," and "Double Loop Learning in Organizations."

WARREN G. BENNIS is a Distinguished Professor of Business Administration at the University of Southern California and Chair of the Advisory Board of Harvard University's Center for Public Leadership. He is also the author of more than 25 books on leadership, creative collaboration, and organizational change.

JAMES BRANT is an organizational sociologist and has joined Mercer Delta Consulting.

TIMOTHY BUTLER and JAMES WALDROOP, both psychologists, are principals at Peregrine Partners, a consulting firm in Brookline, Massachusetts, that specializes in executive development and employee retentions. They are the creators of CareerLeader, an Internet-based career assessment program (careerleader.com), and the authors of *Discovering Your Career in Business* and *The Twelve Bad Habits That Hold Good People Back*.

NATALIE SHOPE GRIFFIN continues to work with Nationwide Financial and other clients as the President of NSpire Leadership, LLC, a leadership consulting firm based in Columbus, Ohio.

JOHN HAMM is an executive coach and leadership trainer based in Los Altos, California. Previously, he was a partner and management consultant at Redpoint Ventures, and prior to that, CEO of Whistle Communications, a technology firm acquired by IBM in 1999. He can be reached at johnhamm@mac.com.

JIM LOEHR, ED.D., is CEO of LGE Performance Systems. Author of 13 books, including *The Power of Full Engagement* (with Tony Schwartz), his pioneering work in performance psychology has been recognized worldwide.

TONY SCHWARTZ is Executive Vice President of LGE and the author of *What Really Matters: Searching for Wisdom in America* and *Work in Progress* (with Michael Eisner).

MELVIN SORCHER has a Ph.D. in psychology and is an organizational psychologist. He remains in private consulting practice.

ROBERT J. THOMAS is Director of the Accenture Institute for Strategic Change, based in Cambridge, Massachusetts. He is the author of *What Machines Can't Do*, *Geeks and Geezers* (with Warren Bennis), and is currently working on a new book describing how organizations can use crucibles to grow leaders.

NOEL M. TICHY is a Professor at the University of Michigan Business School in Ann Arbor. The ideas in this article are explored in his book *The Cycle of Leadership* (with Nancy Cardwell). He can be reached at tichy@umich.edu.

JAMES WALDROOP and TIMOTHY BUTLER, both psychologists, are principals at Peregrine Partners, a consulting firm in Brookline, Massachusetts, that specializes in executive development and employee retentions. They are the creators of CareerLeader, an Internet-based career assessment program (careerleader.com), and the authors of *Discovering Your Career in Business* and *The Twelve Bad Habits That Hold Good People Back.*

Index